The *MLA Handbook* Is Now Available Online.

Buy access online at **www.mlahandbook.org** and start using it today. A print copy will be mailed to you.

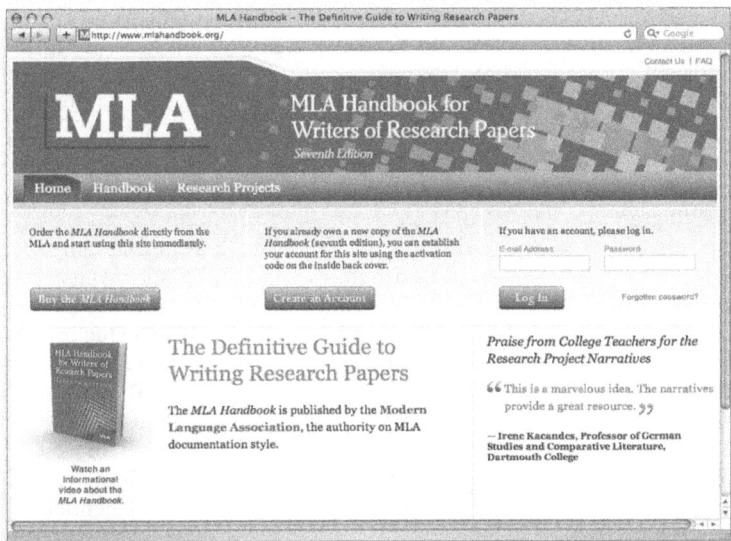

Recipient of *Choice* Award for Outstanding Academic Title

Searchable Web site features

- the full text of the *MLA Handbook*
- over two hundred additional examples
- research project narratives, with sample papers

You can also buy the print edition. An access code in the back allows you to use the Web site, too.

xxii & 292 pp.
Paper 978-1-60329-024-1
$22.00

LARGE-PRINT EDITION
Paper 978-1-60329-025-8
$30.00

Join the MLA and receive 20% discount.

Modern Language Association · **MLA** · 646 576-5161 ■ Fax 646 576-5160
www.mlahandbook.org

Visit the MLA's channel on YouTube at www.youtube.com/user/ModernLanguageAssoc

Reviewers

All essay submissions are reviewed blind by two external readers; those listed below are members of the active reader pool. We thank them for their critical contributions to scholarship in the field.

Linda Adler-Kassner	Lynée Lewis Gaillet	Dan Meltzer
Tom Amorose	Alice Gilliam	Laura Rose Micciche
Valerie Balester	Maureen Daly Goggin	Susan Miller
Cheryl Ball	Angela González	Ruth Mirtz
Nicholas Behm	Lorie Goodman	Clyde Moneyhun
Patricia Belanoff	Heather Brodie Graves	Roxanne Mountford
Patricia Bizzell	Roger Graves	Gerald P. Mulderig
Bill Bolin	Paul Hanstedt	Joan A. Mullin
Darsie Bowden	Dana Harrington	Joddy Murray
Colin Brooke	Jeanette Harris	Marshall Myers
Robert Brooke	Cynthia Haynes	Gerald Nelms
Nancy Buffington	Paul Heilker	Jon Olson
Beth Burmester	Carl Herndl	Peggy O'Neill
Paul Butler	Anne Herrington	Derek Owens
Mary Ann Cain	Brooke Hessler	Irv Peckham
Carol Lea Clark	Charlotte Hogg	Donna Qualley
Kirsti Cole	Bruce Horner	Ellen Quandahl
Lisa Coleman	Rebecca Moore Howard	Kelly Ritter
James Comas	Sue Hum	Duane Roen
Juanita Rodgers Comfort	Brian Huot	Randall Roorda
Thomas Deans	James Inman	Blake Scott
Jane Detweiler	Asao Inoue	Ellen Schendel
Ronda Leathers Dively	Rebecca Jackson	Carol Severino
Sidney Dobrin	T. R. Johnson	Wendy Sharer
Whitney Douglas	Judith Kearns	Steve Sherwood
Donna Dunbar-Odom	Martha Kruse	Donna Strickland
Lynell Edwards	bonnie kyburz	William Thelin
David Elder	Mary Lamb	Peter Vandenberg
Janet Carey Eldred	Donna LeCourt	Deirdre Vinyard
Michelle Eodice	Neal Lerner	Zachary Waggoner
Heidi Estrem	Carrie Leverenz	Kathleen Welch
Sheryl Fontaine	Min-Zhan Lu	Nancy Welch
Helen Fox	Brad Lucas	Thomas West
Tom Fox	William Macauley	Katherine Wills
Christy Friend	Tim Mayers	Rosemary Winslow
Richard Fulkerson	Lisa McClure	Vershawn Ashanti Young
Catherine Gabor	Moriah McCracken	Janet Zepernick

Member of the Council of Editors of Learned Journals

composition STUDIES

Volume 39, Number 1
Spring 2011

Editor
Jennifer Clary-Lemon

Book Review Editor
Asao B. Inoue

Production Editor
David Elder

Editorial Assistants
Christopher Campbell
Bronwyn Jerrett-Enns

Former Editors
Gary Tate
Robert Mayberry
Christina Murphy
Peter Vandenberg
Ann George
Carrie Leverenz
Brad E. Lucas

Advisory Board

Linda Adler-Kassner
Eastern Michigan University

Tom Amorose
Seattle Pacific University

Chris Anson
North Carolina State University

Valerie Balester
Texas A&M University

Robert Brooke
University of Nebraska, Lincoln

Sidney Dobrin
University of Florida

Lisa Ede
Oregon State University

Paul Heilker
Virginia Polytechnic Institute and State University

James Inman
University of Maryland University College

Laura Micciche
University of Cincinnati

Peggy O'Neill
Loyola College

Victor Villanueva
Washington State University

THE UNIVERSITY OF WINNIPEG

SUBSCRIPTIONS

Composition Studies is published twice each year (May and November). Subscription rates: Individuals $25 (Domestic) and $30 (International); Institutions $75 (Domestic) and $75 (International); Students $15.

BACK ISSUES

Some back issues are available at $8 per issue. Photocopies of earlier issues are available for $3.

BOOK REVIEWS

Assignments are made from a file of potential book reviewers. To have your name added to the file, send a current vita to the Book Review Editor at asao@inoueweb.com.

SUBMISSIONS

All appropriate essay submissions will be blind reviewed by two external readers. Manuscripts should be 3,500-7,500 words and conform to current MLA guidelines for format and documentation; they should be free of author's names and other identifying references. *Electronic submissions are preferred*: consult our Web site for details. (For print submissions, submit three titled, letter-quality copies with a cover letter including the title and author contact information, loose postage sufficient to mail manuscripts to two reviewers, and a #10 SASE for the return of reviewer comments.) *Composition Studies* will not consider previously published manuscripts. We discourage the submission of conference papers that have not been revised or extended for a critical reading audience. Those wishing to submit Course Designs should first consult our Web site for specific instructions. Letters to the editor and responses to articles are strongly encouraged.

To ensure a blind review, *Composition Studies* requests
 1. The authors of the document have deleted their names from the text, with "Author" and year used in the references and endnotes, instead of the authors' name, article title, etc.
 2. With Microsoft Office documents, author identification should also be removed from the properties for the file (see under File in Word), by clicking on the following, beginning with File on the main menu of the Microsoft application: File > Save As > Tools (or Options with a Mac) > Security > Remove personal information from file properties on save > Save.
 3. With PDFs, the authors' names should also be removed from Document Properties found under File on Adobe Acrobat's main menu.

Direct all correspondence to:
 Jennifer Clary-Lemon, Editor
 Department of Rhetoric, Writing, and Communications
 University of Winnipeg
 515 Portage Avenue, Winnipeg, MB R3B 2E9
 Canada

Composition Studies is grateful for the generous support of the Dean of Arts and the Department of Rhetoric, Writing, and Communications at the University of Winnipeg.

© Copyright 2011 by Jennifer Clary-Lemon, Editor
ISSN 1534-9322

www.compositionstudies.uwinnipeg.ca

composition STUDIES

Volume 39, Number 1
Spring 2011

**Special Issue:
Wo/men's Ways of Making It in Writing Studies**

editor's note — 9

articles

"What Would Happen if Everybody Behaved as I Do?": May Bush, Randall Jarrell, and the Historical 'Disappointment' of Women WPAs — 13
   Kelly Ritter

Mothers' Ways of Making It—or Making Do?: Making (Over) Academic Lives In Rhetoric and Composition with Children — 41
   Christine Peters Cucciarre, Deborah E. Morris, Lee Nickoson, Kim Hensley Owens, and Mary P. Sheridan

On Not "Making It In Composition" — 63
   Robert Danberg

Narrating Our Lives: Retelling Mothering and Professional Work in Composition Studies — 73
   Loren Marquez

course design

Reimagining "English 1311: Expository English Composition" as "Introduction to Rhetoric and Writing Studies" — 87
   Todd Ruecker

book reviews

Mestiz@ Scripts, Digital Migrations, and the Territories of Writing, by Damián Baca. — 113
   Valerie Balester

The Future of Invention: Rhetoric, Postmodernism, and the Problem of Change, by John Muckelbauer. **116**
    Trisha Red Campbell

Genre in a Changing World, edited by Charles Bazerman, Adair Bonini, and Débora Figueiredo. **119**
    Kerry Dirk

Copyright Clarity: How Fair Use Supports Digital Learning, by Renee Hobbs. **123**
    Kerrie L. Carsey

Decolonizing Literacy: Mexican Lives in the Era of Global Capitalism, by Gregorio Hernandez-Zamora. **126**
    Rebecca Lorimer

Engaging Audience: Writing in an Age of New Literacies, edited by M. Elizabeth Weiser, Brian M. Fehler, and Angela M. González. **130**
    Matthew Ortoleva

Democracies to Come: Rhetorical Action, Neoliberalism, and Communities of Resistance, by Rachel Riedner and Kevin Mahoney. **133**
    Rebecca Richards

Organic Writing Assessment: Dynamic Criteria Mapping in Action, by Bob Broad, Linda Adler-Kassner, Barry Alford, Jane Detweiler, Heidi Estrem, Susanmarie Harrington, Maureen McBride, Eric Stalions, and Scott Weeden. **137**
    Janet S. Zepernick

Going Wireless: A Critical Exploration of Wireless and Mobile Technologies for Composition Teachers and Researchers, edited by Amy C. Kimme Hea. **140**
    Ronda L. Wery

Walking and Talking Feminist Rhetorics: Landmark Essays and Controversies, edited by Lindal Buchanan and Kathleen J. Ryan. **144**
    Nancy Myers

contributors   148

Editor's Note

Erratum: Please note Marta Hess's review of Working in the Archives *appeared in prior issue 38.2; this review was not authored by Leigh Herman as indicated.*

In March 2010, I received an e-mail query from Lee Nickoson asking "if *Composition Studies* might ever consider publishing a special issue on balancing family life and professional life as rhet/comp faculty." Nickoson mentioned in that e-mail the impetus for her request: a 2010 CCCC roundtable centered around responses to Michelle Ballif, Diane Davis, and Roxanne Mountford's 2008 book *Women's Ways of Making It in Rhetoric and Composition*.

I received that e-mail while still on one-year maternity leave with my then seven-month-old daughter and in the midst of preparing my tenure file for review. Having eagerly read—and likely modeled—Ballif, Davis, and Mountford's text when it was first published (and lamenting that I had not had access to such a manuscript when I was in graduate school and on the job market), I took another look. As I trekked to weekly baby groups, read manuscripts to send out for review, and muddled through constructing tabs on an oversized three-ring binder, I thought a lot about what it means to "make it" in rhetoric and composition: to become and to thrive as a professional, as Ballif, Davis, and Mountford say, and to "have a life, too." Thanks to Nickoson's query, *Composition Studies* issued a CFP on "Wo/men's Ways of Making It in Writing Studies" that asked scholars to explore traditional and non-traditional ways of "making it" in the profession; to historicize women's and men's ways of "making it" in writing studies; to explore the intersections of race, gender, and disability in "making it" in the field; to explore "making it" in the context of mentoring, pedagogy, and research. What I realized—only in retrospect—is this (clear, I'm sure, to most): simply issuing a call is no guarantee of the kinds of content you receive in return. As this issue shows, the dialogue scholars want to have about "making it" overarchingly points to the silences that have long-plagued us: we want to talk about what it means to work in a field that consumes us, and choose to parent children at the same time. As reviews have noted, the scholars who are profiled in *Women's Ways* are, in the majority, women without children. It comes as little surprise, for example, that most scholars are familiar with Sondra Perl's oft-anthologized "The Composing Processes of Unskilled College Writers" that appeared in RTE in 1979, but that few cite, as Danberg does, her 1998 piece "Composing a Pleasurable Life." "Composing" makes love, life goals, and dirty diapers a core part of a life that involves the writing classroom—a "lively, exciting, challenging, demanding, nurturing, intellectual space" (251).

Of course, this isn't the only topic contained in this special issue. In "'What Would Happen if Everybody Behaved as I Do?': May Bush, Randall Jarrell, and the Historical 'Disappointment' of Women WPAs," Kelly Ritter explores narratives of disappointment that emerge out of historical revision of women WPAs. Her piece both recovers lost voices and questions the master narrative of the field of Composition Studies in relation to the rise of creative writing as a field of study. Ritter's argument provides a thoughtful framework—to capture the forgotten narrative, to take disappointment as a starting place—for the remainder of the pieces in this issue.

Christine Peters Cucciarre, Deborah E. Morris, Lee Nickoson, Kim Hensley Owens, and Mary P. Sheridan offer five such narratives in their piece "Mothers' Ways of Making It—or Making Do?: Making (Over) Academic Lives In Rhetoric and Composition with Children." The authors offer alternatives to "making it" outside of the R1, tenure-track paradigm while pointing out the limits to myths of "individual choice." Their many narratives of success often take as their exigence flickers of disappointment: moments of imbalance, the dismissal of non-tenure track or adjunct appointments as a path to "making it," the equation of non-tenure track with "the baby track," the minimalization of family commitments to construct a persona of professional success, departmental climates that expect the invisibility of children as a prerequisite of the job. In reimagining what it means to "make it," the authors also invite CS readers to tell their own stories of professional success, in order to contribute to a more diverse composite of those who work in the field.

Robert Danberg similarly recaps how his decisions to parent affected potentialities for professional successes in his piece "On (Not) 'Making it in Rhetoric and Composition.'" His piece synthesizes the choices we make (and that are made for us) as we seek to balance creative work, the work it takes to raise children, and the work that will pay bills on the one hand with the value of scholarly work (represented here, and for many, as both research and the struggle to obtain the PhD) on the other. The ways in which he moves through these moments is not a metaphor of enlightenment, but one of distraction inherent in the struggle to "make it," narrowly defined.

In "Narrating Our Lives: Retelling Mothering and Professional Work in Composition Studies," Loren Marquez offers a final narrative that suggests a changing face and body of those who "make it" in rhetoric and composition. She argues that as more of us in the field strive to make over the common narrative that work and home are truly separate spheres, the more we will contribute to a changing visibility and definition of our "work"—encompassing rich elements of human life outside of the limitations of teaching/research/service.

I'm not sure what I expected when I issued the CFP for this Special Issue, but I do know that I was surprised at the kinds of responses that it elicited. I was concerned, too, that the emphasis placed by contributors on parenting might alienate readers. As one reviewer mentioned, strict focus on mothering specifically "presents a limited construction of what it means for a woman in the field to 'have a real life.'" The reviewer rightly questioned the positions not shown in this issue: "many women [and men] who, by choice, circumstances, or physical constraints/disability, don't have children." Another reviewer asserted, "I am uncomfortable with another expression of gender rights that isn't further along than portraying a middle-class family archetype, Mother, as an ideal to be preserved in the face of having 15 million people out of work now . . . [these realities] might re-write that ideal or at the least historicize it." Both of these reviews reflect ways in which "making it," particularly in the face of a radically-changed economic climate, has been problematized even in the three short years since *Women's Ways* was published (and counting the one to two years it likely spent in press). Even my own decision, like Marquez's, to have a child while on the tenure track, cannot be discounted by the fact that I live in a country that afforded me with 95% of my take-home pay while on maternity leave, and three months of Employment Insurance for my partner to take a leave of absence from work to stay home with our newborn. Our stories of "making it"—in traditional ways or otherwise—often mask the undercurrents of social realities: the job you had to take or the job that never emerged, the health problem that forced you into a decision, the real estate market that created a choice for you. It is my hope that the pieces published here offer a snapshot of the ways in which "making it" depend very much on the available means one has at the time to do so. I hope to continue here dialogue prompted by *Women's Ways* and encourage us to imagine diverse ways of "making it" in writing studies, and a shared commitment to equity and balance in our work-life and life-work practices.

Within the pages of this Special Issue you will see features both familiar and new. Todd Ruecker's Course Design "Reimagining 'English 1311: Expository English Composition' as 'Introduction to Rhetoric and Writing Studies'" offers ways in which we might re-see existing FYC courses as introductions to Writing Studies within the constraints of traditional approaches. A new cover celebrates *Composition Studies'* thirty-ninth year in press. I've chosen the image of a compass to represent the ways in which writing studies, broadly conceived, offers both a center location and a place of navigation for scholars working in the field.

Works Cited

Perl, Sondra. "Composing a Pleasurable Life." *Women/Writing/Teaching*. Ed. Jan Zlotnick Schmidt. Albany: SUNY P, 1998. 239-54. Web. 9 Feb. 2011.

Rhetoric & Writing PhD Program

Celebrating Our Thirtieth Anniversary in 2010!

Since its founding in 1980, Bowling Green State University's program has prepared more than eighty graduates for faculty careers in rhetoric and composition. Students and faculty in the Rhetoric & Writing PhD Program are committed scholar-teachers who utilize a range of approaches—rhetorical, cultural, empirical, technological—that characterize rhetoric and composition in the twenty-first century.

Some highlights of the Rhetoric & Writing PhD Program:
- Eight core courses in history, theory, computer-mediated writing, research, scholarly publication, and composition studies as a discipline, plus electives in rhetoric and composition and related areas of scholarly interest to students.
- Professional development involving mentoring, collaboration, a monthly colloquium series, and post-prelim groups emphasizing dissertation work and the job search.
- Varied assistantship assignments (FYW, intermediate writing, writing center, faculty research, editorial work, program administration, community outreach, etc.) and competitive non-service fellowships in the fourth year of funding.
- Four-year graduation rate typical for full-time students.
- 100% placement rate among program graduates.

Rhetoric & Writing PhD Program
http://www.bgsu.edu/departments/english/rcweb/index.html
Facebook Group: BGSU Rhetoric and Writing Program

Program Director, Richard Gebhardt
richgeb@bgsu.edu
English Graduate Office 419-372-6864

"What Would Happen if Everybody Behaved as I Do?": May Bush, Randall Jarrell, and the Historical 'Disappointment' of Women WPAs

Kelly Ritter

> The feminized labor of Composition Studies is usually seen as being in service of, or subservient to, literary studies, ignoring Composition's disaffective position against other fields, specifically creative writing. Viewing Composition Studies' complex labor histories in tandem with the meteoric rise of creative writing allows for a new way of historicizing writing instruction and writing program administrator successes and failures. Analyzing WPA work through an archival case study of one woman's college faculty postwar, specifically the WPA May Bush and the poet Randall Jarrell, illustrates how the disciplinary rise of Composition and Rhetoric against creative writing was fraught with gendered labor issues still relevant to the struggles of women WPAs today.

In "More than a Feeling: Disappointment and WPA Work," Laura Micciche notes the under-theorized "climate of disappointment" that pervades the personal narratives and day-to-day experiences of writing program administration. Micciche argues that an open discussion of this disappointment, using a framework of emotion and affective performance, is critical to achieving better social and material conditions for WPAs. Almost all of Micciche's example narratives of disappointment in her article belong to women—not surprisingly so, as Composition Studies generally and WPA work specifically is notably "feminized" (see for example Sue Ellen Holbrook's "Women's Work," Susan Miller's *Textual Carnivals*, and Eileen Schell's *Gypsy Academics*). Micciche closes her article by opining "whether, en route to hope, we can speak candidly about professional inequities and disappointments without being regarded as doomsayers, as spoilers of the democratic identity that composition studies has constructed of itself" (454-55).

I want to augment Micciche's charge by acknowledging that narratives of disappointment are difficult to voice, precisely due to the overwhelmingly positive (and perhaps *positivist*) view of Composition Studies as a site for social and intellectual change. To admit to individual or collective failures within this mission is tantamount to ethical sacrilege. If we were to welcome this contrarian analytical framework for viewing WPA work, however, and also take this view of "disappointment" in a more *historical* direction, we might subsequently rediscover two often-elided elements of Composition

Studies' master narrative. One such element is the collective lost voices of WPAs who worked at women's public, regional colleges where disappointment was a real—if undocumented—aspect of professional life, in contrast to the more positive (and widely disseminated) narratives of women WPAs at the Seven Sisters colleges.[1] Another less tangible, and perhaps therefore less-examined, element is the cultural phenomena that affected the work of women WPAs beyond those accepted within our disciplinary lore, i.e., the collapsing job market, the proliferation of contingent labor, and the devaluing of the humanities (Micciche 432). This phenomenon is the rise of creative writing as an academic field of study, a postwar event that put curricular and intellectual stress on the previously singular notion of "academic" writing, namely composition, as well as on composition's labor force and administrators.

I contend that we should re-examine the historical narratives of women WPAs who didn't "make it," in part, to acknowledge the larger disciplinary and departmental circumstances that led some of these WPAs' work to be eclipsed by the rising star of creative writing courses and faculty. Such recasting of the WPA labor story in a new disciplinary context is critical to expanding our current understanding of the historical work of Composition Studies *and* creative writing, as well as the ongoing gendered nature of first-year writing instruction and program administration. We typically view the feminized labor of Composition Studies as being in service of, or as subservient to, literary studies, while ignoring composition's very real disaffective position in academia more generally, particularly as set against the attractive and culturally revered field of creative writing. To see Composition Studies' complex and often disappointing labor histories in *tandem* with the comparative meteoric rise of creative writing—a field that de-emphasized the conscripted "labor" of writing in favor of curricular and intellectual "artistry" in writing (literature) production—allows for a new perspective on how we have historically conceived of writing instruction and program administration successes and failures, writ large, at the postsecondary level.

There is a historical disciplinary tension between creative writing and composition that belies its current allied-discipline status present in the literature of Rhetoric and Composition Studies and made explicit in certain pedagogical approaches (for example, process theory). While today we see the relationship between creative writing and composition to be, in some departments, nearly seamless, we should be cognizant of the very different and very real economic and curricular impulses that led to the rise of, and historical conflicts between, these two fields of writing instruction. To position the WPA figure at the center of that tension is all the more critical, and logical, when we recognize the past and continued feminization of Composition Studies—a feminization that does not seem to be consistently associated with creative writing as a field. Is this because the work of writing program administration is seen as the supreme example of "women's" work? Is the difference instead rooted in the masculine tradition of the misunderstood artist, the impractical soul who holds students' rapt attention but cannot be concerned with more minute matters of day-to-day budgetary or curricular issues?

In response to these two questions, I employ a case study of writing and WPA work at a public women's institution mid-century, the Woman's College of the University of North Carolina. By dissecting archival evidence of the parallel—but clearly unequal—career trajectories of two Woman's College faculty who serve as personifications of the tension between creative writing and composition, Professor May Bush, WPA, and Professor Randall Jarrell, prominent poet and MFA program architect, I demonstrate that the disciplinary rise of creative writing against Composition and Rhetoric is indeed fraught with gendered labor issues relevant to the struggles of women WPAs, and is thus a story that needs to be added to the history of WPA work in our field, in order to augment our existing aggregate perspectives. I aim in my examination to encourage readers, particularly fellow WPAs, to undertake similar small-scale studies that will uncover additional, and perhaps competing, narratives of women's (WPA) work on other overlooked campuses, including, perhaps, their very own. So long as the field of Composition and Rhetoric continues to be highly dependent upon the goodwill of (women) scholars to run writing programs, while in contrast, the field of creative writing is far less dependent upon compulsory "management" constructions for its aggregate faculty, the relevance of uncovering and linking together individual histories of the divergent models of "work" between these two fields is an enterprise that needs to be encouraged and practiced via the examination of local archives and relatable, human examples.

The History of Composition is a History of Its People: WPA Narratology

If we accept the premise that the history of Composition Studies is a history of its people, people who can speak for themselves as well as those who must be spoken for through archival interpretations, it becomes clear that the voices of women who *didn't* "make" it are key to understanding the larger narrative of the field of Composition Studies today. The historical narratives of women WPAs are peppered with failure, secondary to fierce competition for both program resources and professional recognition, and a diminishing institutional status for first-year composition, a course that prior to World War II had been a prodigious site for providing literacy-based acculturation to a homogeneous (white, male) college populace. As postwar populations shifted, however, making space for minority and female students to enter these classrooms, the figure of the WPA began to be troubled in both its conception and its mission. Whereas earlier decades of writing instruction emphasized the solidification of class and status-based ideologies via writing instruction, as Sharon Crowley and Robert Connors have each illustrated, the postwar era emphasized rote assimilation of marginalized student-types into the status quo, and employed strategies emphasizing efficiency over edification in order to do so.

In addition to this shift in what it meant to teach and, consequently, administer writing, the postwar era ushered creative writing into college settings as a venue within which undergraduate and graduate students could broker a new and attractive merger of "academic" writing and literary appreciation, as has been examined by both Joseph Moxley and D.G. Myers in their historical studies. This emergence of creative writing as a hybrid subdiscipline within English studies exacerbated the already-tenuous status of the WPA, who found herself no longer in charge of a singular definition or dissemination of writing instruction on campus. Suddenly, the WPA was in competition with a viscerally appealing curriculum steeped in "artistic" aims. This postwar emergence of creative writing may be the true origin of composition's association with "lesser" ways and means today, inasmuch as composition thereafter failed to achieve a similar public patronage and institutional admiration, and was subsequently reduced from an art to a "skill" for study. Along with this contrasting disciplinary standing for first-year composition and rhetoric came the lowered visibility of the WPA herself.

As other scholars of Composition Studies have noted, the figure of WPA through the 1960s is a shadowy one. English departments did not always give these men and women an official title, nor did they bestow upon them any extra compensation. The early WPA typically exists as a beleaguered and bitter paper-pusher assigned the intractable task of overseeing freshman courses that students did not want to take and faculty did not want to teach. As was articulated in the October 1964 report of the CCCC Workshop on "Administering the Freshman Course":

> Several representatives deplored the fact that most experienced members of the faculty wish to withdraw from teaching Freshman English as soon as they can. Some reported that their schools make Freshman English more palatable by . . . giving credit toward promotions and salary increases to those who distinguish themselves in teaching Freshman English . . . Most participants agreed, however, that these and other devices have done little to lessen the belief that Freshman English is a drudgery which the experienced teacher will abandon as soon as he can. (197)

This lingering impression of composition teaching and administration as undervalued and lacking in meaningful institutional recognition is in sharp contrast to that of creative writing faculty, who are charged with teaching and sometimes overseeing attractive, elective courses that enroll eager students. In this 1964 report, we see a familiar mid-century lament: teaching freshman English is neither intellectually satisfying nor practically tenable, in terms of the work (reading, grading, commenting) required. We see a preview of the split in place in the twenty-first century, where upwards of 80% of first-year writing at the postsecondary level is assigned to contingent faculty, often the less "experienced" among us (graduate students, for one). In contrast, we rarely (if ever) see a similar lament about the undergraduate teaching of poetry or fiction writing; these courses are usually seen as a plumb assignment, a reward rather than a burden, despite their similar labor-intensive qualities (reading and commenting upon multiple pieces of writing) and lower-level position in the curriculum. Instead, the evaluation of creative writing is seen as an engagement in improving *art*, a far more mysterious, master-apprentice-based model than composition's (perceived) rote corrective methodologies.

Unlike creative writing—which has its roots in the 1940s in terms of formalized graduate degree programs and has ancestors prior to that, especially in non-academic settings wherein poets and novelists worked with writers' colonies, retreats, and other extra-curricular groups—Rhetoric and Composition was not a field of graduate study until the mid-1970s. Because this field is thus a relative latecomer to academia, early WPAs were almost without exception scholars and teachers of literature, often with no particular training in, or inclination toward, program administration, and with no community for professional support, as Amy Heckathorn has argued in "Moving Toward a Group Identity." Historically speaking, the narrative of the WPA is not an uplifting one; however, this story is typically told in the absence of cultural phenomena, with the assumption that Composition Studies' only "enemy" was literature. In fact, the rise of creative writing postwar posed perhaps the deepest threat to Composition and Rhetoric, and the WPA figure, in its presentation of a more palatable form of writing now available both inside *and* outside academia.

The rise of creative writing on college campuses creates a more dire paradigm for the WPA than existed prior to 1945, when the first graduate programs in writing emerged and the field exploded. As Mark McGurl has documented in his recent book, *The Program Era*, in 1945, just two years before the Woman's College hired Randall Jarrell to join its faculty, there were only eight MFA or MA programs in creative writing in existence nationwide; these were at the University of Iowa, Stanford University, University of Florida, Indiana University, University of Denver, Cornell University, Johns Hopkins University, and Boston University. By 1965, not long after the MFA at the Woman's College was formalized, just ten more institutions—Brown, Columbia, Virginia, Oregon, Massachusetts, Syracuse, UC Irvine, Montana, USC, and Washington University–St. Louis—had joined these ranks (25). Yet only one of these total eighteen programs—the MFA at the University of Virginia—was in the Southern United States; the remainder were clustered in the upper Midwest, the Northeast, and on the West Coast. Additionally, none of these MFA programs were housed at current single-sex colleges or universities (ignoring for the moment that Brown and Columbia did not admit women, and were thus single-sex *male* institutions, in their earlier years), nor did any have the history of educating women, or for that matter, *teachers*, that the Woman's College possessed. These institutions with MFA programs were all either flagship state universities or prominent private colleges and universities. So for the Woman's College to embark on first, an expanded creative writing focus in its English department, and second, an MFA program, in the context of these other national models was, indeed, a revolutionary step that would put the college squarely on the map where graduate study in the arts was concerned.

But the Woman's College foray into graduate instruction in creative writing postwar was not necessarily a unique request in the context of colleges nationwide, despite the revolutionary move for women's graduate education that its initial program proposal constituted. By 1975, in fact, there were 52 institutions in the United States with MFA programs in creative writing; that number had grown to 83 programs by 1999 (Bishop and Starkey 117). In 2009, that number was 153 (Fenza). These statistics evidence a 84% increase in programs between 1999 and 2009—indicating, perhaps, a second wave of creative writing popularity in post-secondary institutions—and a 300% increase in number of programs between 1975 and 2010. Thus, one may observe that while doctoral studies has experienced a comparative stagnation, due to an unsure job market in academia and a general decline in funding for less visible or financially profitable PhD programs (such as religious studies, philosophy, and, more recently, American Studies) the MFA in creative writing is, and historically has been, one of the fastest-growing graduate specializations in the humanities in the United States.[2] The MFA, unlike the PhD, has historically served the dual purpose of drawing writers/artists into the academy when they might otherwise eschew such a restrictive setting, and calling the public's attention to the academy as a patron of the fine arts.

The growth of the MFA may be traced to several more specific impulses related to this dual purpose of politics and aesthetics, as situated within English departments such as the Woman's College postwar. One of these impulses was to reinforce the notion of writers as living, breathing entities rather than historical figures, which was to reify the English department as a colony of working writers passing on their trades, in real time, to students. As stated on the main page for the Associated Writing Programs (AWP), the organization notes that in the mid-1960s, "on most campuses, the best, most respected writers were those long dead and safely entombed in anthologies and libraries," and thus AWP was founded to support the growing presence of literary writers in higher education. Because, at that time, Departments of English were mainly conservatories of the great literature of the past, scholars fiercely resisted the establishment of creative writing programs. To overcome this resistance and to provide publishing opportunities for young writers, AWP was founded by fifteen writers who represented twelve writing programs. (Fenza)

The apposition here of "writers" and "scholars" is telling, as it signals the root division of creative writers as artists versus literature scholars as academics/researchers/non-artists. Such a stance, however, glosses over the position of Composition and Rhetoric, or in curricular terms, the enterprise of rhetoric and expository writing, within this paradigm. Indeed, the meteoric rise of creative writing has been documented in relation to literary studies, and as either the root of, or the inspiration for, more expressivist tendencies in Composition, particularly the use of the "workshop" model for peer review of student writing, and the multiple-draft, pure-process pedagogy of early 1970s composition scholars such as Kenneth Bruffee, Donald Murray, and Peter Elbow. But the politics of creative writing versus composition is in large part under-theorized, despite the clear declarations from the AWP about the identity of the writer as exclusively the *creative* writer, i.e. the poet or novelist, or perhaps playwright—not the writer of expository works or rhetorical criticism. As R.M. Berry notes, "as the academic contact with political and economic power has increased, Creative Writing has been in the thick of things while theory has remained aloof . . . . Despite a generation of critical theories insisting on the historical situatedness of all literary practice, literary criticism still treats the institution for forming American writers as a world apart" (58). Because this philosophical separation exists, creative writing "is less likely to consider itself a sub-specialty of literary scholarship than to *define itself in contrast to* literary scholarship" (Berry 66, emphasis added). A similar separatist philosophy exists when one seeks out a disciplinary history of creative writing in relation to Composition Studies more generally, even when there is an explicit attempt to marry the pedagogical concerns and pursuits of these two related fields.

The WPA figure, as the administrative representative of composition within the university, was a relatively unproductive and unknown scholar and figure compared to the creative writing faculty member, existing at the intellectual margins and working outside the realm of the non-academic public. In addition to having less cultural clout, WPAs were identified not by their intellectual work, but by their association with management and paper-pushing tasks, particularly when it was commonplace for a literature faculty member to occupy the WPA role. WPAs were not expected—nor were often inclined—to produce scholarship *about* composition. There were few outlets for such scholarship anyway, as Maureen Daly Goggin has observed, since early articles in field journals "pose[d] no argument, interpretation, evaluation, or critique . . . [but] explain[ed] in narrative form a practice or process in which the author engaged" (46). WPAs were assigned duties in administration, sometimes as part of a rotation, sometimes by the short straw, and very often prior to tenure, without hope of connecting their scholarship to their administrative duties. By comparison, the faculty who taught in creative writing programs were, by universal requirement, prolific writers themselves, publishing their own work to institutional accolades, selected as administrators not for any reason beyond their writing talents, but for ability to draw attention to the program. These administrators also did not face the structural, budgetary, or other personnel issues endemic to large-scale composition programs. They were already typically separated from the daily duties of the English department by a separatist curricular philosophy, as noted above, and were responsible for oversight of either a menu of elective courses or a concentration positioned beside, but not necessarily beholden to, either literature or composition.

While narratives of creative writing program directors are scarce[3] and lore-based stories of program directors exist through self-studies of prestigious programs,[4]—itself a problem facing historians who wish to integrate labor narratives of creative writing and Composition in meaningful ways—scholars of Composition Studies have begun to compile historical evidence of some particular WPA's working conditions. The most comprehensive collection of these narratives is L'Epplatenier and Mastrangelo's *Historical Studies of Writing Program Administration,* wherein contributors reinforce the common instigating image of the undertrained, undervalued, and exhausted WPA. *Historical Studies* profiles WPAs at Bryn Mawr and Vassar, and also discusses the influential 1919 meeting of WPAs from Mount Holyoke, Wellesley, and other Seven Sisters institutions, but does not profile any public women's institutions such as the Woman's College. Mastrangelo and L'Epplantenier argue that the networking done by these elite school WPAs "refutes the notion that these women, like so many other participants in rhetoric and composition's history, were individual actors, toiling in isolation, with little or no support from those around them" (118).

At the Woman's College, however, May Bush did appear to be an "individual actor." Her story exemplifies the social and material consequences of being a woman program administrator in the era of a male-centered creative arts movement. At the Woman's College, creative writing grew exponentially, and raised the profile of the institution further with its MFA program, while composition comparatively fell. At the same time, the disciplinary notion of "feminization" in writing instruction interestingly cut both ways. As women students at the college were being trained to be inquisitive, independent thinkers and writers—if sometimes still being educated within a patriarchal paradigm that ensured their social growth be somewhat inhibited by strict campus rules and regulations[5]—their fellow women *faculty* were receiving far less intellectual attention and recognition by comparison. This is a field paradox that unwittingly enacts Micciche's observation of "an exacting bitterness, or disappointed hope, in what the academy has become and failed to become" (433).

A Tale of Two Promotions: May Bush and Randall Jarrell

As the only public women's college in the state, the Woman's College of the University of North Carolina (since 1964 known as the co-educational University of North Carolina-Greensboro, or UNCG) sought and maintained a separate and specialized identity within the UNC system for over seventy years.[6] It fiercely held to founder Charles McIver's original decree that "When you educate a man, you educate an individual; when you educate a woman, you educate a family." The college deeply believed in its promise to produce women graduates of intelligence and taste. It resisted threats of extinction for many years from the men's campus at Chapel Hill, and going into the postwar era prided itself on the niche it filled in the South as the pre-eminent institution of its kind. The rise of creative writing as a field of study—already represented in college course listings since 1930, evidencing an early recognition of the widespread popularity of the field that was to come mid-century—combined with the college's history of excellence in women's education, allow it to argue, postwar, that its English department was a unique regional foothold worthy of any national adversary.

Such conditions enabled the appearance of an MFA program in the early 1950s, since, as D.G. Myers argues, creative writing was perhaps the most successful of all disciplines in allowing women a greater writerly agency, a goal that matched McIver's. This agency was clearly contrary to the growing notion that composition was "women's work" and that theme correction was an arduous task that discouraged positive connection between writer and text, or text and teacher, and thus was the province of women—as a housekeeping act not worthy of men's time. In contrast to this negatively feminized work, creative writing allowed women to be not only *teachers* of writing but also *producers* of literary work—ergo *art*—themselves, and to be recognized both inside and outside the academy. This artistic production, as part of our culture's valuation of the author as mystical star, was far more attractive than pursuits of any professional kind in composition.

Myers also notes that creative writing shifted literary study from the "past to the present" (140), providing women with a chance to become a part of a growing body of evolving work-for-study, and further, the opportunity of practical criticism, which "desexed literature by inverting the categories and values of the older literary and educational establishments" transforming literature into an "impersonal constructive technique" that did not discriminate (140). Indeed, Katherine Adams contends that between 1880 and 1940,

American women came to college to learn to be writers. They took advantage of every opportunity to form groups of colleagues, and they continued to rely on this model after they left college, creating new types of personal/professional groups. And from this home base, they crafted very influential texts that helped shape their era. (xviii-xiv)

Adams emphasizes the woman writer as one who sees writing, especially imaginative or creative writing, as a legitimate *vocation*, a career possibility that created a bridge between postsecondary institutions and the "real" world of reading, writing, and community literacy. We can see this viewpoint enacted in the Woman's College publications of first-year writing, *The Yearling* (initiated by May Bush herself, in 1948) and the literary magazine *Coraddi*, which operated outside the English department as an extracurricular club. The grassroots origins of these publications positioned women students as the architects of literacy collectives, with the idea that they would spread their talents across their home and work communities, becoming "teachers" in a figurative (and sometimes literal, for education majors) sense.

Indeed, Adams notes that even though women's colleges, starting in the 1920s, were reducing their offerings in dance and theatre, creative writing offerings were generally not cut, as they were a combination of "academic study and arts practice" (42). As early as 1915, colleges such as Smith and Barnard were offering a much wider range of creative writing courses than their elite men's counterparts, who lagged behind this movement for some twenty years (Adams 51). Notably, Adams does not include *public* women's colleges, where such creative work was also thriving, in her study. But these positive benefits of creative writing for women students had no administrative correlation for the Woman's College WPA. Her separation from literary studies, like the required course that she governed, served to annex her from any writerly agency. This stands in contrast to the poet Jarrell, whose intellectual separation from literature *increases* his agency. Using a sports metaphor to illustrate this situation, if Jarrell was a sought-after free agent, Bush was the last-round draft pick.

"Surely You Have Enough About Me!": May Bush

Little is known about May Bush, and that in itself is telling. As opposed to the boxes of Jarrell's archival papers housed in the UNCG library, May Bush has just one slim folder. Bush came to the Woman's College in 1934, with an artium baccalaureus (A.B.) from Hollins College and an MA from Columbia University. She taught high school in Greensboro from 1924 to 1926, at Finch College (NY) from 1926 to 1932, and at Peace College (NC) from 1934 to 1935 ("Two To Retire"). At the bottom of her final 1960-1961

"Biographical Information" form, dated October 10, 1960, Bush added a handwritten comment: *"Surely you have enough about me!"*

Perhaps Bush's frustrated missive reflects the fact that while she had completed this same form four times during her tenure, her answers had hardly changed. Bush had published one article on Milton concomitant with receiving her doctorate, but in the space for "Titles of published works" she never lists it, nor is it mentioned in her retirement announcement. Between coming to the Woman's College in 1934 and retiring in 1968, Bush received her PhD from Johns Hopkins University in 1942, allowing a promotion to assistant professor after eight years of instructor rank. In 1952 she would be promoted to associate professor, and in 1960, to full professor.

The only archival prose about May Bush comes from a brief, published eulogy written by departmental colleague Amy Charles, and a letter written by a later department head on the occasion of Bush's death. At Bush's retirement from the university in 1968, Charles noted:

> Miss Bush's students have commended her insistence of high scholarly standards for herself and for them, her fair-mindedness, her enthusiasm, and her belief in them. Colleagues have mentioned her unflagging concern for excellence, her courage and integrity, her steadfastness and lack of self-seeking, and her utter honesty. New instructors have had reason to appreciate her friendly welcome, her instinctive kindliness, her grace and dignity, as well as her awareness of practical difficulties that more than once has led to loans to tide over the newcomer awaiting his first pay day.

We can see Bush's feminine traits ("grace and dignity") being highly valued here, in contrast to the sometimes-rough or isolationist portrait of the typical (male) writer—think Hemingway, Faulkner, any canonical male author held up as a writerly ideal. Indeed, her apparently outgoing nature and enthusiasm would stand in some contrast to widely accepted portraits of Randall Jarrell, often characterized as a "loner" and supremely private individual, dedicated to his craft. It is ironic that one of Bush's noted traits would also be generosity, given her own financial difficulty throughout her career; Jarrell, in contrast, is not characterized as stingy, but is known for his love of sports cars, bought with his considerable Woman's College salary.

Charles closes her piece by recalling Bush's lifelong ethical principle, advanced by her philosophy professor at Hollins College: *"What would happen if everybody behaved as I do?"* This question seemed to drive her polite acceptance of her lesser departmental status. It also provides a haunting meta-question for this article, and my inquiry into postwar women's WPA work: What, indeed, *would* have happened if everyone at the Woman's College "behaved" as May Bush did, and failed to get on the lucrative bandwagon of creative writing when it burst onto the academic scene? Or, what would have happened if composition had been a more forceful presence in the

English department, and in the English departments of other colleges like the Woman's College, and had been recognized as a scholarly subject in the 1940s rather than the 1970s? Would this story of professional disappointment and denied promotions for women WPAs, and for women laboring in Composition Studies in general, instead be one of accomplishment and advancement, across department sub-fields, and genders?

Chairman Robert Stephens repeats Bush's philosophical mantra in his letter to her two sisters in 1983, insisting

> It is good now to remember her as she was during her long active career on this campus, as a fine and conscientious teacher and adviser, as a responsible member of this department and this faculty, who set high standards for her students and for herself . . . . May had a rare quality of thinking of others first . . . . She opened the eyes of her students to learning . . . she always took more than her share of the responsibility.

Stephens makes no note of Bush's scholarship—which, admittedly, was minimal—and instead focuses, like Charles, on Bush's personality and ethics. She is the good soldier; she is the one who took "more than her share" while being given far less in return. She is the martyr for a variety of unpopular departmental causes, among them composition, left unstated here. While very little in the archives narrates Bush's accomplishments, in fact, her presence at department meetings was regular and her contributions always noted respectfully, in a department that had its own personnel tensions and unique women colleagues. Bush is not in the league of Professor Nettie Sue Tillett, whose behavior was frequently characterized as disruptive or inflammatory, and whose actions were critiqued by Randall Jarrell himself.[7] Nor is she comparative to Lettie Hamlett Rogers, who resigned her position over the chancellor's censure of a nude sketch (drawn by an art student) in the literary arts magazine *Coraddi*. Additionally, Bush cannot by definition have kinship with the first and second Mrs. Jarrell—who were tied to their husband and thus purely contingent labor, yet given pay raises more often than Bush was herself.

Despite her heavy service load, May Bush was keeping up with the profession—in her case, the literary profession, and its relevance to school teachers. In the December 13, 1954 minutes it is noted that Bush would attend that year's MLA; Bush also appears in several notes in the *South Atlantic Bulletin,* citing her work for the North Carolina Education Association, which articulated and refined secondary school English requirements for the state. Stephens notes further in his letter that Bush "worked hard to see that younger colleagues were promoted and that older ones were honored for their accomplishments." It is notable to recall that each of the institutions where Bush was employed—Finch, Peace, and the Woman's College—were women's institutions, as was her undergraduate alma mater (Hollins College in Virginia). Thus, Bush had a personal commitment to women's education that was clearly visible, a commitment that extended to her junior women colleagues. But despite these selfless beliefs, her own road to promotion and tenure was troubled.

While a skeptic might point to Bush's lack of scholarship as rationale for her lack of timely advancement in rank and pay, an archival reading of Bush's situation highlights two issues that undercut this argument. First, a lack of publications would be a logical consequence of being assigned heavy administrative (and committee) duties in first-year writing and general education, on top of a 4/4 teaching load; unlike Jarrell's notably lighter teaching load of two courses per semester, there is no indication that Bush had any reassigned time for her administrative work. Second, the fact that her English department chairs continually advocate for her advancement—but these words of advocacy fall on deaf ears at the level of the dean, who grants similar requests regarding Randall Jarrell—show that Bush's department supported her promotion (and tenure), or at least articulated such support in chair's reports, and thus held her in a position of some use value during her tenure at the Woman's College.

Archival department records are thick with a long history of requests for Bush's promotion (and tenure), articulated, in some cases, multiple times from department head Leonard B. Hurley to the higher administration. These requests are located in the papers of the chancellors and deans to whom the appeals were made, and are also alluded to in some departmental documents related to personnel matters and faculty accomplishments. The first notable request comes on March 23, 1948, as Hurley writes to Chancellor Jackson to appeal for two "urgent cases"—one of which was May Bush. Hurley categorizes these requested increases in salary as *the* two to be made "if <u>any</u>" should be funded for Fall 1948:

> Dr. May Bush is completing her fourteenth year at the Woman's College. Since coming here she has spent two years in graduate study at Johns Hopkins University and has been awarded her PhD degree with distinction by that great university. She is an extremely hard and conscientious worker and an excellent scholar. She is very highly regarded in the English department and throughout the College and the community. She serves as Chairman of the Freshman English work—a taxing job. She teaches Freshmen, Sophomores, Juniors, and Seniors . . . . Dr. Bush is on the Board of Trustees of Hollins College and could go there to teach at any time she made known her desire to do so. (I know that there is an opening there for her next year). Dr. Bush wishes to stay at Woman's College, but I think that she is becoming pretty thoroughly discouraged because she has had no promotion in rank during the past eight years.

This would be the first in many requests from Hurley, a staunch, classically-trained and traditional-thinking literature professor who (by alumna accounts) kept a firm leash on the department and an even firmer leash on the women students and faculty, seeing himself as a kind of father figure to all. Despite Hurley's predilections as chair, however, he defends Bush's work and her value to the department and college, recognizing the personal toll the numerous denied promotions have taken on her. While Hurley, as gleaned from other department archival documents, seems quite conservative and even occasionally overbearing, his advocacy for Bush is undeniable.

On June 9, 1948, Hurley sends a follow-up memo to Jackson, noting that Bush receives $3360 annually, and that "if nothing more can be done at this time, [her salary] must be brought to at least $3500.00 . . . . It will take only . . . $140.00 to do this." In April 1949, Hurley reiterates his previous request word-for-word, and adds that "I have been urging [this] for four years." He also re-articulates the need for promotion to full professor for faculty Rowley and Gould—women associate professors who had been at this rank for twenty-six and twenty-two years, respectively. At this point it seems prudent to ask: to what degree was the lack of promotion and advancement for Bush due to not only her lesser-status as a teacher and director of composition, but also her gender? Was the progressive view of the Woman's College toward its students, and their intellectual advancement as writers, in fact not adequately reflected in its views toward women writing *faculty*? The answer seems to be that both gender and teaching/administrative area may have been a factor.

In an English department report for the year 1964-65, an accounting of current departmental faculty by rank is spelled out in detail by then-English chair Dr. Joseph Bryant for then-dean of the college Dr. Otis Singletary. In this report, May Bush is listed as one of the five full professors in the department, having finally achieved this rank in 1960-61. However, Bush and her colleague, Dr. John Bridgers—a faculty member whose vocal concerns for first-year and basic writing are noted in numerous department meeting minutes, and whose teaching was primarily at the freshman and sophomore levels only—are simultaneously singled out as those who "cannot be qualified to direct theses in the graduate program," and are relegated as for "undergraduate" teaching only. Because, as noted in the report, Bush and Bridgers are not able to direct MA theses, this leaves only two (male) professors—Bryant and Watson—eligible to potentially do so at the full professor level. A third associate professor, Dr. Jean Gagen, is described as having published her first book through a "vanity press"; the report notes that she may come up for promotion concurrent with Dr. Watson, on the strength of a second book "now nearing completion." However, Bryant's November 1961 memo makes clear that Watson would be the preferred choice of the two, as "putting him [Watson] in competition for a position with Miss Gagen would [be] for many reasons . . . unfortunate" as his "value to the Department is considerably greater." This value is never articulated;

his only two distinctive qualities separating him from Gagen, however, are his gender, and his status as a creative writer and protégé of Jarrell. One may interpret this report to read that not only were composition-primary faculty valued less than literature-primary and especially creative writing faculty, as weighted by their perceived ability to direct graduate theses, but also that male faculty were being valued over women faculty.

A review of department standards for promotion and tenure during this postwar era reveals no specifics on these two cases, however—as such matters are typically not part of the public record and many comments on individual cases are never recorded. But the evaluation form is somewhat telling in its categories which may make the promotion of men—and creative writers—more likely. In addition to the rank, salary, and years in service, faculty are rated as "Excellent," "Superior," "Average," or "Inferior" based on (1) Teaching Ability (with no subheadings); (2) Personal Traits, with the subheadings of Intellectual Integrity, Breadth of Interests, Emotional Balance, Cooperation, and Open-Mindedness. There are also two blank spots for additional write-in subheadings within this category; (3) Administrative Ability; (4) Professional Growth, with subheadings of Research, Creative Work, Professional Activities, and Further Study; and (5) Service to Campus, Community, State, and Nation (Faculty Evaluation form).

One notes that while teaching is first, "personal traits" is second—ranked above Administrative Ability, Professional Growth, and Service. It is hard to ignore that this nebulous category includes "emotional balance," which surely could have been used to single out women. May Bush, by all indications, smartly resisted this "emotional" profile in her departmental work, and was implicitly rewarded for this resistance by Hurley, but faculty such as Nettie Tillett clearly did not. In addition, "cooperation" serves as an early term for the oft-contested current notion of "collegiality," another point in which gendered power relations within a department could certainly result in a low ranking. It is hard to know how "open-mindedness" is to be read, but one possible interpretation is the acceptance of new (unwanted) duties without complaint. Within an institution that valued women's abilities—as *students*—to enter into society with a range of knowledge and a keen sense of self and community, it seems ironic that such standards would exist in the review of women *faculty*.

Further, it seems odd that given the low status of "research" in this paradigm—a subheading under "professional growth," low on the form—certain faculty would be singled out for their lacking scholarly production (such as Bush, barred from directing MA theses, and Gagen), while the creative writers would be lauded for their own publishing accomplishments.[8] Here, we begin to see discordant evidence: even though the teaching load was quite high, and much scholarship thus not necessarily expected, the creative writing faculty were significantly—perhaps inordinately—valued *for* this production, work that was not only part of their "professional growth" but also public evidence of their standing as productive artists. Their high production level also allowed the department to excel in one corner of creative production—original poetry and fiction—and thus over-achieve within the typical framework of a teaching-centered, regional college for women, wherein the woman WPA had one of the highest work burdens of all faculty.

May Bush would carry the legacy of her WPA workload through her career at the Woman's College, staying on faculty despite her disappointing road to full professor. In a memo dated April 12, 1957, from Dr. Hurley to Dean Mereb Mossman, Hurley outlines Bush's venerable track record in his larger request for Bush's promotion to full professor, the sole subject of the memo. He recalls her many accomplishments inside and outside the college, including her work as "chairman" of Freshman English (again labeled as "taxing"); and her departmental committee work; her university service on the College Chapel Committee, the War Bond Drive, and the Committee on Humanities in General Education. Hurley also notes Bush's service to local organizations such as the Guilford County Mental Hygiene Society and her membership in the MLA, SAMLA, AAUW, and other regional professional organizations. He concludes that she is a "well prepared, scholarly, and most conscientious teacher . . . something of a leader in the intellectual life of the community. I think she deserves the promotion requested."

But this promotion was not to be, as evident by Hurley's subsequent memo to Dr. Gordon Blackwell, Chancellor, on March 5, 1958. Hurley articulates his past request for May Bush's promotion, and later in the memo more fully spells out his underlying concerns, in institutional context:

> The Department of English at the Woman's College has had for many years at least one woman at full professorial rank (See attached material). In recent years we have had two women professors. Both retire this year. I think that in a women's college, in every department staff that includes a number of women, as the English department here does, there should be at least one woman with the rank of Professor. Dr. May D. Bush will be the top ranking woman in the department . . . . I hope that she may be promoted at this time.

Hurley's archived material on rankings and gender indicates exactly the proportion that he here broadly describes. The latest year charted was 1951-1952, in which two of the nine full professors were women; in both 1943-1944 and 1946-1947, one of the eight full professors was a woman. In these earlier years of the college, before budgetary conditions and curricular impulses favored creative writing, there was consistently one woman full professor among the five to eight full professors listed. Such disparity is evident in one of the last salary comparison sheets for the Woman's College during

May Bush's employment. In 1960-1961, Randall Jarrell's salary is $10,500. Leonard Hurley's salary as head is only $9,200 by comparison. Bush, having finally achieved full professor in Fall 1960, has a salary of $7,500, the lowest of all full professors. Robert Watson, an associate professor, has a salary of $6,700—just $800 behind May Bush, despite her service record extending sixteen more years. Add to this accounting the fact that Bush went with *no* raises of any kind from her appointment to assistant professor in 1940 through 1945, and one can see the demoralizing frame around her career.

The main two creative writing faculty in the department during this era—Randall Jarrell and Peter Taylor—were to be away on leave, quite frequently for one or more semesters at a time. The report thus deduces that given these conditions, neither could bear the administrative responsibility of day-to-day program tasks that May Bush did. Jarrell's personal papers alone contain at least twenty letters from universities and colleges pleading for visits and public readings on their campuses to occupy his time. These requests were frequently lucrative; in 1956, Oglethorpe College offered Jarrell $750 for one day's work—one-tenth of his then-yearly salary. May Bush would receive no such offers or public recognition, her past offer of employment from Hollins College notwithstanding. As a WPA and faculty member associated with service and, arguably, servitude, Bush would never be singled out as valuable to the *prestige* of the college—a factor important in promotion and retention decisions. Jarrell, in contrast, would spend his nineteen years at the Woman's College living a celebrated life known only to prominent poets and fiction writers, at the college he would come to call "Sleeping Beauty."

"They Leave You to Yourself Extraordinarily": Randall Jarrell

Randall Jarrell's collected letters illuminate his institutional standing and highlight the material differences between being a creative writing faculty and being a WPA, as well as being a male faculty member versus a female faculty member, during the postwar era. Jarrell was hired into the Woman's College as an associate professor, despite having only an MA, while his first wife Mackie was hired as an instructor. Jarrell's letters evidence that Mackie's appointment was not based on any particular qualifications besides being his wife, and that Randall's rank was barely justifiable, given that he had only taught for three years at the University of Texas at Austin, and for one year at Sarah Lawrence prior. This illustrates Jarrell's critical material difference from May Bush, who had to wait eight years for a promotion to associate professor, even with a doctorate.

Indeed, Jarrell's early correspondence with fellow writers such as Robert Lowell characterizes university teaching as an especially good "gig" for a writer, with fairly light work expectations. Jarrell writes to Lowell in October 1947:

> I have seven girls in my writing-poetry and fifteen in my modern poetry . . . The classes are better than I thought they'd be—quite serious and overjoyed with the poetry . . . . Wouldn't you like to come next year to take my job for a year . . . ? You'd have a job with the rank of associate professor, a good bargaining point from which to arrange for another job; there'd be very little work and $3600; they leave you to yourself extraordinarily . . . .

Jarrell's letter to Lowell evidences his low teaching load and lack of compulsory commitments to the college. The notion that the college "leave[s] you to yourself extraordinarily" right away signals a different expected work ethic between Jarrell and Bush. Whereas May Bush was lauded for her undying devotion to the department, and her students—an almost monastic existence, at least on paper—the creative writer, as represented by Jarrell here (or, potentially, Lowell) is allowed a fair amount of latitude in terms of expected departmental service/contributions as well as a notably small amount of students to teach. A comparative look at Jarrell's load against that of May Bush shows a clear imbalance: in Spring 1955, for example, Jarrell had 11 students total, all in upper-division courses, whereas May Bush had 80, 70 of whom were lower-division. Hurley's own accounting for the "average" faculty load from this same semester indicates a figure of 79.5 students, nearly identical to Bush's load, but far above Jarrell's.[9] Jarrell did not teach freshman writing, nor was he expected to do so. Jarrell's differential teaching load status seems somewhat shocking in retrospect, especially considering other contemporary factors at the college, such as high enrollment caps of 25 to 28 students in first-year composition and heavy lower-division loads carried by Bush and other women and junior faculty in the department.

This is not to say that Jarrell did not enjoy his teaching. He once famously stated that "Teaching is something that I would pay to do, to make my living by doing it, here . . . with the colleagues I have and the students my colleagues have" (453). Upon his return to the college in 1953, after a two-year absence, he exclaimed, "Gee, I'm glad to be back here. This college is like Sleeping Beauty" (387). Of course, one might argue that it is relatively easy to enjoy teaching when one has fewer than twenty students per term, and is teaching elective courses that are highly attractive to students, particularly aspiring young women writers already personally invested in the arts. In fact, Randall Jarrell enjoyed semester and year-long teaching positions at several other colleges, and upon each of his returns, enjoyed a rewarding financial perk of some kind, to add to his already-revered status in the department and on the larger campus.

Jarrell's starting salary, as noted by Dr. Hurley, was at the top of the associate professor scale: $3600. Still, Jarrell was wondering about future salary increases and promotion in rank, as articulated in Hurley's April 1947 letter—which is archived in Randall Jarrell's personal papers at UNCG, and which also evidences Hurley's explicit promise to make money no object in future negotiations:

> You will note that those who fixed the salary for the newly created position which we have offered Mr. Jarrell fixed the salary at the top of the bracket for Associate Professors according to the old [contract] . . . it is pretty well fixed for next year . . . . Hence I have attempted to see to it that the figure for Mrs. Jarrell's salary is near the top [$2400.00] . . . so as to even this up as much as possible. I cannot make definite commitments for the future; all that I can say is that we are most eager to build up our writing group within the department and that *I will do all within my power toward this end.* (emphasis added)

As feverish as Hurley had advocated for Bush's pay raises, his tone is clearly more laced with desperation in his pleas for Jarrell's financial standing in the college. He even is willing to argue for a top-flight pay scale for Jarrell's wife who, if archival records are any indication, brought nothing specific or special to the department other than her status as the spouse of a coveted writer. The archives reveal that Hurley made good on his promise to "do all within [his] power," thereby safeguarding, in the department's view, the future of creative writing at the Woman's College. In the years between his 1947 appointment and his untimely 1965 death, Jarrell was wooed from the outside with great rigor, and the English department at the Woman's College struck back repeatedly, at the expense of other personnel. One such strike from Dr. Hurley to Dean Walter B. Jackson comes in May 1949, as part of a dual-request memo for salary increases for both Peter Taylor and Jarrell. Hurley notes that "If $4200 could be provided for Mr. Peter Taylor, we could bring him back" next year, and that "Mr. Taylor was receiving $3500.00 . . . . A 15% increase on this would bring the sum to $4025.00. An additional sum of only $175.00 would provide the necessary $4200.00." It is notable that the salary increase is construed somewhat of a bargain, and granted; similar "bargain" requests for Bush during this same era were repeatedly denied.

Despite these pay raises, Jarrell secured a temporary leave from the college from 1951 to 1953, teaching first at Princeton University, and then at the University of Illinois. Following this leave, the most striking example of anxiety regarding Jarrell's future at the Woman's College comes in a lengthy handwritten letter from Leonard Hurley to Chancellor Gordon Blackwell on January 25, 1958, addressed to Blackwell's vacation home in Ithaca, New York. The letter, excerpted below, details Jarrell's offer from Kenyon College and exemplifies the frantic prospect of Jarrell's departure from the Woman's College, as well as the subsequent demise of the creative writing program:

> When Randall arrived at Kenyon a few days ago, he was told . . . that they wanted to offer [the editorship of the *Kenyon Review*]. The salary stated was $10,000—but I believe John Crowe told Randall that they might go slightly higher. He was to teach one class, to work with the young writers, and to edit the *Review*. Mr. Jarrell . . . felt that he must give the offer very serious consideration, but is apparently not too eager to accept it. He spoke of how much he liked his work and his associations here in Greensboro . . . I gather the idea, too, that he feels that desirable as it would seem in many ways to be at the head of the influential *Kenyon Review* [but] the editorial work involved . . . would leave him less free for his own writing than the work here has done . . . . I would like to emphasize: I think Randall Jarrell is in all probability the person of greatest national reputation and distinction in our teaching faculty, and one imminently suited to working in our faculty. He very much likes teaching young women, and his students like him . . . . We should not lose Jarrell if any means can be found by which he can be kept here as a center around which we can rebuild our writing program.

As evidenced here, Jarrell was explicitly the present and future of the Woman's College *itself.*

Hurley draws a portrait of a beatific writer and man who resists uprooting himself and his family, but is torn by professional opportunities. In today's university, of course, careers are made and broken over competing employment offers. But Hurley makes it clear that Jarrell's future is not simply his own: his national reputation is the cornerstone of the creative writing program itself. Ultimately, Hurley's appeal was successful; Jarrell remained at the Woman's College, with a substantial bump in pay. In retrospect, what was a coup for the Woman's College, and for Jarrell personally, was the beginning of a successful narrative of creative writing at the college that exists to this day, and a local example of the pressing cultural forces that pushed Composition and Rhetoric out of the leadership role in college-level writing for arguably the better part of the remaining years of the twentieth century. This contrasts with our current conceptions of both Composition and creative writing as symbiotic sub-fields, growing and changing in harmony with one another and breeding similar pedagogies—such as the "workshop" model and the very idea of peer review—that both struggle to claim, but share amicably. This portrait of Bush against Jarrell also contradicts the notion that the disappointment of WPA work of which Micciche speaks, specifically for women, is a relatively recent, freestanding phenomenon independent of the trajectories of other fields of writing. Such contrasts and contradictions are critical to include in the histories of labor in Composition Studies, and in the still-evolving portrait of the twentieth century WPA.

Women's Working Legacies: The Anti-Hero

In their introduction to *Women's Ways of Making it in Rhetoric and Composition,* Ballif, Davis, and Mountford quote a survey respondent as remarking, "women in our field have been absolutely heroic . . . against significant odds" (3). In this book, several prominent women scholars of Rhetoric and Composition are profiled, such as Patricia Bizzell, Cheryl Glenn, and Andrea Lunsford. Certainly there is good reason to celebrate these extraordinary women and their many accomplishments. But the notion of the "heroic" woman who occupies the role of scholar/teacher/administrator in Composition Studies represents only one facet of the field's history, and *Women's Ways* profiles explicitly the most heroic of those heroes, so to speak, since Composition Studies emerged in the 1970s. Just as Jeanne Gunner, in "Iconic Discourse," argued for a reconsideration of the basic writing teacher as hero, so, too, should we strive to more deeply contextualize what it means to "make it" (or *not*) in the historically-contested field of WPA work. We should examine our narratives of failure just as closely as we seek to emulate our narratives of success, particularly when these narratives cause us to re-examine previous disciplinary alliances and historical conditions for labor, such as those facing Composition and Rhetoric postwar.

In my pursuit of this wider characterization of women's WPA work, contradictions between women's literacy education and the treatment of May Bush at the Woman's College, including her own low-cost salary and denied promotions, complicated my own viewing of both the relationship between creative writing and composition in the academy and the real possibilities of women's administrative labor within even specialized (single-sex) educational spaces. Of course May Bush's story—of a local, shoulder-to-the-wheel nobody who would never aspire, or be selected, to appear in a collection such as *Women's Ways*—might be argued as an isolated narrative in history, neither representative of the trajectory of women's labor in Composition Studies nor the cultural valuation of creative writing over composition. This is an easy argument to make at the moment, since no other WPA narratives or histories that I have found contextualize this work in terms of the rise of creative writing in the academy. I would, therefore, call for other scholars to do similar readings of their local archives, to historicize their own institutions' writing program administrators against their other programs in English, particularly those public institutions with MFA programs either past or present, and/or with histories of providing an education for women.

As a singular case study, however, the Woman's College stands as a negative example of women's advancement that both recalls and advances Micciche's work, and troubles the master narrative of WPA work. What might this contrast between Jarrell and Bush's intertwined careers teach us about the historical roots of interdepartmental relations between Composition and creative writing today—especially those units that have coalesced into independent departments of "writing" set against traditional English departments? The cultural valuation of "artistic" versus "academic" labor that put these two fields historically in competition is one we should consider further as we train, staff, and promote our writing faculty, and graduate students, in each of these disciplinary areas, but especially those who will do administrative labor in writing programs, or who will move from undergraduate or master's degrees in creative writing to doctoral work in Composition Studies. Further, the exploration of local case studies of writing program administration, particularly at atypical/lesser-studied settings such as the Woman's College, highlight the human dimension complicating any standardized notions of "labor" that might otherwise characterize the field, particularly where women's labor is concerned. The Woman's College cannot stand in for *all* mid-century writing program administration, but it can illustrate the local consequences that one extremely prominent creative writing program had on an arguably "average" composition program—one run by a literature faculty who was also a woman. These historical, material conditions surely exist at many other colleges and universities around the country; bringing together an aggregate of these cases would provide a much fuller perspective on both women's labor in Composition Studies and the assumed-prototypical labor conditions of the WPA, particularly during the postwar era's emphasis on "creativity" and creative writing, heretofore imagined as more of an ally than a competitor in the rise of Composition Studies as a field.

As sociolinguist Charlotte Linde affirms in her study of institutional remembering, *Working the Past,* singular and historical narratives can productively disrupt the dominant paradigms shaping any institution, including Composition Studies. Linde notes that "the highest ranked member of the institution" usually tells the story of that institution (203); in Composition Studies, this member is often the external teacher/scholar who narrates the history of a program or programs, or prevalent lore across programs. But that teller is speaking from an elevated external position, and is therefore unable to represent the local; that teller is also re-presenting the most dominant voices, whereas there are also "noisy silences" to be represented, or "silences in one situation about matters spoken loudly or in whispers in other situations" (Linde 197). These are what we commonly refer to as counter-narratives; in Composition Studies, these include the voices of women students and faculty whose stories have not been historically represented in WPA narratives, nor in disciplinary histories of creative writing versus Composition.

We need to hear more about what happened when these women's professional agencies failed, or were sabotaged by circumstances beyond their control, or by otherwise-imagined allied fields such as creative writing which put their scholarship and curricular or administrative work (and use value) in competition for valuable university resources. We are still more likely in our field histories to catalog individual stories of success than individual stories of failure and disappointment, particularly when they expose uncomfortable contention between seemingly overlapping, even friendly, fields such as Composition and creative writing. These "noisy silences" in the history of women's administrative work in Composition Studies are what I represent here, through the long-forgotten tale of Professor May Bush.

Notes

1. See David Gold's book *Rhetoric at the Margins* for a fuller discussion of the importance of recovering the local histories of public women's colleges, as well as HBCUs, within our archival narratives of Composition and Rhetoric. I am indebted to Gold for being the first to call our field's attention to this lack in representation within our scholarship; my larger book project, from which this article is excerpted, discusses Gold's work in slightly more detail.
2. R. M. Berry notes that in 1990, "around 3,000 poets and fiction writers" were graduating from creative writing graduate programs each year, compared with 800 doctoral recipients in other fields of English studies (57).
3. See Sharon Crowley, *Composition in the University*, Chapter Seven, "You Can't Write Writing: Norman Foerster and the Battle over Basic Skills at Iowa." Notable, of course, in this example of an early creative writing program director is Foerster's claim to fame: his vision that creative writing would be an organic outgrowth of the English department, rather than a separate (financial and philosophical) arm of the university, divided from department literacy initiatives and scholarly pursuits.
4. See for example collections such as Tom Grimes's *The Workshop: Seven Decades of the Iowa Writers' Workshop*.
5. Students at the Woman's College were required, for example, to participate in closed study each evening; observe a rule of "lights out" at 11:30 p.m.; and adhere to strict policies against men in the dormitories. Each class wore the standard dress of a skirt and the "class jacket," a blazer with a color combination specific to each year's class. Dining hall meals were served "family style" with an appointed hostess for each table, who enforced proper table manners and was responsible for facilitating conversation within each table of diners. The social atmosphere was, by all accounts, designed to simultaneously promote equity and rotating opportunities for leadership *among* the women, while also promoting the college's secondary mission of producing well-mannered, socially proper young women upon graduation. As such, the college uniquely combined, according to alumna accounts and as is evident in archival documents, the social atmosphere of a finishing school with the intellectual rigor of the Seven Sisters (or other highly selective) colleges.
6. The college was founded in 1892 as a normal school and reconstituted in 1931 as a public women's general college, and since 1964 has been the co-educational University of North Carolina-Greensboro.

7   In the May 14, 1956 minutes, there is an extended statement by Randall Jarrell, which reads, in part:

> I spoke briefly about the problem of Miss [Nettie] Tillett's behavior in staff meetings. My tone was serious, objective, and troubled . . . . I said that, for as long as I had known it, our department had been faced with an extraordinary problem: the problem of having one member who did not observe, in department meetings, the ordinary rules of social behavior, but who allowed herself to make intemperate or openly insulting remarks about the head of the department, the department as a whole, or individual members of the department . . . .

   Tillett resigned from the Woman's College at the end of the 1957-58 academic year; in a January 1958 memo from Mereb E. Mossman, dean of the college, to Chancellor Gordon Blackwell, Mossman ironically notes this resignation alongside Randall Jarrell's return (from leave) to the college for 1958-59, at a projected salary of $7500—a salary equal to Tillett's final salary for 1957-58. Mossman also asks, "how heavily would we be justified in drawing on [a reserve in Romance Languages] to add to Mr. Jarrell's salary?"

8   Gagen's book was published by Twayne Publishers (New York); whether this would be considered "vanity" is somewhat debatable. The press is now an imprint of Gale/Cengage.

9   The low load carried by Jarrell did not go unnoticed by higher administration, though it also appears to go unchanged—and in contrast, is sanctioned—throughout his career at the Woman's College. In a memo to Chancellor Graham on April 21, 1955, Dean Mossman communicates that she "talked with Dr. Hurley about Mr. Jarrell's teaching load and implications of such a small load. He is going to work on this problem with the thought that the poetry class might develop into a considerably larger class and also consider the possibility of a sophomore English section for Mr. Jarrell for the coming year." Note that half of this proposed solution hinges upon Jarrell's poetry class increasing in size—i.e., the growing of the creative writing concentration—rather than a load re-evaluation beyond the possible sophomore English section. His two-course (six-hour) load continued into the 1960s, as is noted in a November 1961 memo from then-department chair J.A. Bryant to Dean Mossman, in which Jarrell's two-course load is referenced in relation to his offering of an advanced graduate seminar at the Chapel Hill campus. Hurley concluded that this seminar should be considered "overload" for Jarrell, and that he thus should be paid "an additional amount equal to one-third of his regular salary for the semester [and] should also be reimbursed for his weekly transportation to and from Chapel Hill." Meanwhile, his fellow colleagues in the English department—those not in creative writing—were teaching a 4/4 load, with no extra pay.

Works Cited

Adams, Katherine H. *A Group of Their Own: College Writing Courses and American Women Writers, 1880-1940*. Albany: SUNY P, 2001. Print.
Ballif, Michelle, Diane Davis, and Roxanne Mountford. *Women's Ways of Making It in Rhetoric and Composition*. New York: Routledge, 2008. Print.
Berry, R.M. "Theory, Creative Writing, and the Impertinence of History." *Colors of a Different Horse: Rethinking Creative Writing Theory and Pedagogy*. Ed. Wendy Bishop and Hans Ostrom. Urbana: NCTE, 1994. 57-76. Print.
Bishop, Wendy, and David Starkey. *Keywords in Creative Writing*. Logan: Utah State UP, 2006. Print.
Bryant, Joseph A. "English Department Staff, 1964-1965." TS. Otis Arnold Singletary Collection. U of North Carolina-Greensboro Archives, Greensboro.
———. Memo to Dean Mereb E. Mossman. 7 Nov. 1961. TS. Otis A. Singletary Collection. U of North Carolina-Greensboro Archives, Greensboro.
Bush, May Dulaney. Personnel Form for News Bureau. 1 Feb. 1941. TS. May Bush File, Biog. Files of Fac. U of North Carolina-Greensboro Archives, Greensboro.
———. Personnel Form for News Bureau. 2 Dec. 1943. TS. May Bush File, Biog. Files of Fac. U of North Carolina-Greensboro Archives, Greensboro.
———. Personnel Form for News Bureau. 10 Oct. 1960. TS. May Bush File, Biog. Files of Fac. U of North Carolina-Greensboro Archives, Greensboro.
CCCC Workshop. "Administering the Freshman Course." *CCC* 15.3 (1964): 197. Print.
Charles, Amy. "May Delaney Bush." *Alumni News,* Spring 1968. TS. Biog. Files of Fac. U of North Carolina-Greensboro Archives, Greensboro.
Connors, Robert. *Composition-Rhetoric: Backgrounds, Theory, and Pedagogy*. Pittsburgh: U of Pittsburgh P, 1997. Print.
Crowley, Sharon. *Composition in the University: Historical and Polemical Essays*. Pittsburgh: U of Pittsburgh P, 1998. Print.
Department of English. Meeting of the Staff Minutes. 13 Dec. 1954. TS. Dept. of English Collection. U of North Carolina-Greensboro Archives, Greensboro.
———. Meeting of the Staff Minutes. 14 May 1956. TS. Dept. of English Collection. U of North Carolina-Greensboro Archives, Greensboro.
Faculty Evaluation Form. N.d. TS. Walter C. Jackson Collections. U of North Carolina-Greensboro Archives, Greensboro.
Fenza, Dave. "About AWP: The Growth of Creative Writing Programs." *The Association of Writers & Writing Programs*. AWP, 2009. Web. 1 Oct. 2010.
Freshman English Class of the Woman's College of the U of North Carolina. *The Yearling*. CN Y39 V 1.1-4.1 (Spring 1948-Spring 1951). Print. U of North Carolina-Greensboro Archives, Greensboro.
Goggin, Maureen Daly. *Authoring a Discipline: Scholarly Journals and the Post-World War II Emergence of Rhetoric and Composition*. Mahwah: Lawrence Erlbaum, 2000. Print.
Gold, David. *Rhetoric at the Margins: Revisiting the History of Writing Instruction in American Colleges, 1873-1947*. Carbondale: Southern Illinois UP, 2008. Print.
Gunner, Jeanne. "Iconic Discourse: The Troubling Legacy of Mina Shaughnessy." *Journal of Basic Writing* 17 (1998): 25-43. Print.
Grimes, Tom. *The Workshop: Seven Decades of the Iowa Writers' Workshop—43*

Stories, Recollections, and Essays on Iowa's Place in Twentieth Century American Literature. New York: Hyperion, 2001. Print.

Heckathorn, Amy. "Moving Toward a Group Identity: WPA Professionalization from the 1940s to the 1970s." *Historical Studies of Writing Program Administration.* Ed. Barbara L'Epplantenier and Lisa Mastrangelo. West Lafayette: Parlor, 2007. 191-220. Print.

Holbrook, Sue Ellen. "Women's Work: The Feminizing of Composition." *Rhetoric Review* 9.2 (1991): 201-229. Print.

Hurley, Leonard B. Fac. Rank by Year for 1925-26, 1929-30, 1934-35, 1938-39, 1943-44, 1946-47, 1951-52. TS. Dept. of English, Woman's College. Gordon William Blackwell rec., 1957-60, UA 2.6, box 6. U of North Carolina-Greensboro Archives, Greensboro.

———. Letter to Chancellor Gordon W. Blackwell. 25 Jan. 1958. TS. Gordon William Blackwell Collection, 1957-1960. U of North Carolina-Greensboro Archives, Greensboro.

———. Letter to Chancellor Gordon W. Blackwell. 5 Mar. 1958. TS. Gordon William Blackwell Collection, 1957-1960. U of North Carolina-Greensboro Archives, Greensboro.

———. Memo to Chancellor Edward K. Graham. 5 May 1951. TS. Edward Kidder Graham Collection. U of North Carolina-Greensboro Archives, Greensboro.

———. Memo to Chancellor Edward K. Graham. 13 July 1951. TS. Edward Kidder Graham Collection. U of North Carolina-Greensboro Archives, Greensboro.

———. Memo to Dean Walter C. Jackson. 23 Mar. 1948. TS. Walter C. Jackson Collection. U of North Carolina-Greensboro Archives, Greensboro.

———. Memo to Dean Walter C. Jackson. 9 June 1948. TS. Walter C. Jackson Collection. U of North Carolina-Greensboro Archives, Greensboro.

———. Memo to Dean Walter C. Jackson. 30 Apr. 1949. TS. Walter C. Jackson Collection. U of North Carolina-Greensboro Archives, Greensboro.

———. Memo to Dean Walter C. Jackson. 10 May 1949. TS. Walter B. Jackson Collection. U of North Carolina-Greensboro Archives, Greensboro.

———. Memo to Dean Walter C. Jackson. N.d. (spring 1949?). TS. Walter B. Jackson Collection. U of North Carolina-Greensboro Archives, Greensboro.

———. Letter to Randall and Mackie Jarrell. 18 Apr. 1947. TS. Randall Jarrell Papers, 1929-69. U of North Carolina-Greensboro Archives, Greensboro.

———. Memo to Dean Mereb E. Mossman. 9 Feb. 1956. TS. Dept. of English Collection. U of North Carolina-Greensboro Archives, Greensboro.

———. Memo to Dean Mereb E. Mossman. 12 Apr. 1957. TS. Gordon William Blackwell Collection, 1957-60. U of North Carolina-Greensboro Archives, Greensboro.

———. Report on English department enrollments and teacher-student loads to Dean Mereb E. Mossman. 27 Oct. 1955. TS. Edward Kidder Graham Collection. U of North Carolina-Greensboro Archives, Greensboro.

Jarrell, Randall. *Randall Jarrell's Letters*. Ed. Mary Jarrell. New York: Houghton Mifflin, 1985. Print.

Linde, Charlotte. *Working the Past: Narrative and Institutional Memory*. Oxford: Oxford UP, 2008. Print.

Mastrangelo, Lisa, and Barbara L'Epplantenier. "Is It the Pleasure of This Conference to Have Another? Women's Colleges Meeting and Talking about Writing in the Progressive Era." *Historical Studies of Writing Program Administration*. Ed. Barbara L'Epplantenier and Lisa Mastrangelo. West Lafayette: Parlor, 2004. 117-144. Print.

McGurl, Mark. *The Program Era: Postwar Fiction and the Rise of Creative Writing*. Cambridge: Harvard UP, 2009. Print.

Micciche, Laura. "More Than a Feeling: Disappointment and WPA Work." *College English* 64 (2002): 432-458. Print.

Miller, Susan. *Textual Carnivals: The Politics of Composition*. Carbondale: Southern Illinois UP, 1993. Print.

Mossman, Mereb E. Memo to Chancellor Edward K. Graham. 21 Apr. 1955. TS. Edward Kidder Graham Collection. U of North Carolina-Greensboro Archives, Greensboro.

———. Memo to Chancellor Gordon W. Blackwell. 26 Jan. 1958. TS. Gordon William Blackwell Collection, 1957-1960. U of North Carolina-Greensboro Archives, Greensboro.

Moxley, Joseph. *Creative Writing in America: Theory and Pedagogy*. Urbana: NCTE, 1989. Print.

Myers, D.G. *The Elephants Teach: Creative Writing Since 1880*. Englewood Cliffs: Prentice Hall, 1996. Print.

Schell, Eileen. *Gypsy Academics and Mother-Teachers: Gender, Contingent Labor, and Writing Instruction*. Portsmouth: Boynton Cook, 1997. Print.

Stephens, Robert O. Letter to Mrs. Russell Lyday and Miss Ellen Douglas Bush. 7 Nov. 1983. TS. Biog. Files of Fac. U of North Carolina-Greensboro Archives, Greensboro.

"Two to Retire." TS. May Bush File, Biog. Files of Fac. U of North Carolina-Greensboro Archives, Greensboro.

Offering M.A. and Ph.D. programs in English, as well as a new Ph.D. program in Rhetoric and Composition, TCU provides students with a tradition of excellence in graduate studies that combines intellectual development with practical training and professional mentoring.

Qualities that draw students to our department:

◊ A nationally respected faculty

◊ Competitive, multi-year fellowships and a 1-1 teaching load for Graduate Instructors

◊ Opportunities for experience working for the New Media Writing Studio

◊ An outstanding record of student placement and publication

To learn more about the programs in rhetoric, composition, and literature at TCU, visit us at

www.eng.tcu.edu

Mothers' Ways of Making It—or Making Do?: Making (Over) Academic Lives In Rhetoric and Composition with Children

Christine Peters Cucciarre, Deborah E. Morris, Lee Nickoson, Kim Hensley Owens, and Mary P. Sheridan

> This article focuses on five women's experiences "making it" as rhetoricians with children. Expanding the definition of success Michelle Ballif, Diane Davis and Roxanne Mountford set forth in *Women's Ways of Making It in Rhetoric and Composition,* the article offers suggestions for moving toward more family-friendly academic structures, not least by recognizing that the seemingly individualistic idea of choice—such as the choice to have children—rests uneasily with the often invisible structures that shape and delimit choices. The authors call for increased visibility of and acceptance for a greater range of possibilities for "making it" in the field today.

This article, a hybrid of academic and personal prose, gives voice to the experiences of a varied group of women rhetoricians with children. We read Michelle Ballif, Diane Davis, and Roxanne Mountford's *Women's Ways of Making It in Rhetoric and Composition* and found their definition of success generally skewed toward Research I schools and toward women without children.[1] We think there are more ways of "making it," and more women "making it" with children, than that focus makes visible. Here, then, we widen the lens by describing our ways of meeting or exceeding professional expectations as academics who are also mothers. As a group, we are able-bodied, white, straight academic women with children whose experiences have varied considerably. Our range is not exhaustive, but includes being a single, adoptive parent on the tenure track, being a returning graduate student with nearly-grown children, and being securely tenured with school-age children. Three of us had children while we were graduate students; two of us experienced the job market as nursing mothers. One of us eschewed a tenure-track path to focus on teaching and her child, a decision that both delights and haunts her. We haven't had the same paths; we haven't made the same choices; we have, however, each confronted the notion of succeeding as a faculty member and together and separately have come to see that the definition offered in *Women's Ways of Making It,* which at present speaks for our field, requires expansion.

What follows, then, is a series of reflections—narratives of our individual experiences contextualized within research on work-life balance in academia. Although it is unlikely any of us would say we have mastered the work-life balance (if such a mastery is even possible), as mothers we can agree that care-giving responsibilities—perhaps particularly for young children—make the sum of the work-life (im)balances reflected in *Women's Ways* unlikely models. Several profiled scholars mention twelve-hour work days and/or seven-day work weeks, practices which are generally unsustainable—and undesirable—for mothers of young children. Consequently, we offer these snapshots with hope that they might help broaden the range of possibilities of how we achieve work-life balance as Rhetoric and Composition scholar-teachers in the field today.

Finding A Way: Achieving (Moments of) Life-Work Balance
Lee Nickoson

Ballif, Davis, and Mountford describe the aim of *Women's Ways of Making It in Rhetoric and Composition* as telling the myriad stories of women faculty who have achieved public notoriety for their contributions to the field—women rhetoricians singled out as examples of successful teacher-scholars—as "models for other women in the profession who aspire to 'make it,' too: to succeed as women academics in a sea of gender and disciplinary bias and to have a life, as well" (3). Reading this statement of purpose left me wondering about all sorts of things: what do the authors and the 142 women who responded to the survey on which their discussion is grounded consider to be professional success? How do these many women colleagues understand—and how have they experienced and successfully (or not) navigated the waters of—disciplinary subjectivities? Is there any correlation between any of our various subject positions as women in the field (rank, type of home institution, race, gender, age, etc.) and how we understand and enact the work-life balance? I found myself most eager to learn more about the status of women in the field and, in so doing, to perhaps learn more about how and where I fit.

I had many epiphanic moments while reading *Women's Ways of Making It*. I found myself attaching Post-it after Post-it to pages where I wanted to come back and spend more time considering particular findings. The most profound insight I gleaned from Ballif, Davis, and Mountford's discussion, though, came early in a chapter aptly titled "Searching for Well-Being: Strategies for Having a Life." In it, the authors argue that we need to redirect our energies and, rather than asking "How can I have a life while doing this job?" they posit that women faculty who reported feeling a sense of satisfaction in their lives instead ask, "How can I find a balance that sustains me?" (165).

Balance. *Women's Ways* concludes with narrative profiles of nine Rhetoric and Composition scholars whom survey respondents identified as representing women who have made it. One of those profiled, Lynn Worsham, describes her effort to achieve balance. "Balance," Worsham comments,

> is an ongoing process; sometimes you have more and sometimes you have less. It's important to know what is necessary to your well-being and to your sense of yourself, what your limits are, and how to say no. 'Having a life' or finding balance requires that you know at least these three things. (317)

For me, that balance involves the professional and the personal, which I find translates to: teaching, advising, and mentoring both undergraduate and graduate students; engaging various short- and longer-term research scholarly projects; and participating thoughtfully and as fully as possible as a member of my department, college, university, and disciplinary communities. And, for me, the personal translates to parenting my daughter, participating as a member of my church and local community, and sustaining and growing my relationships with family and friends. As far as achieving balance, I feel I am and likely will be for some time a work in progress, which I find is one of the lead challenges of the balancing act—the realization that balance is not, and cannot be, a once-and-forever static experience. Rather, I understand achieving balance as an effort to inhabit a state of mental and emotional equilibrium—an attempt to achieve steadiness of mind and soul. I've come to know that I can't always maintain that equilibrium, and that that is okay. Rather, I experience blissful, contented moments of balance, and it's those moments, I find, that energize and sustain me. The challenge for me, then, becomes finding ways to experience those moments of steadiness as often and as fully as possible.

Some moments of equilibrium, I've learned, can be anticipated, such as those short periods of time when my five-year-old Olivia and I walk across campus on Monday, Wednesday, and Friday afternoons when we make the short trek from the car to the university's laboratory preschool. Those ten-minute walks are a highlight of my week. They serve as regular and yet powerful reminders of how fortunate I am—fortunate to have a job in such dire economic times, let alone enjoy a career in the profession I have, since I was young, wanted to join. And now I have the opportunity to share that part of my life—my self—with my daughter. We have some of our best conversations during those short walks, too: I learn about her day, and, if I'm lucky, I might get to hear her sing the university fight song once, twice, or ten times. Most importantly, though, I find our walks are moments in which we get to be in each other's public lives—we get to experience life on a university campus together. I spend the time between when I drop Olivia at preschool and when I pick her up three hours later one building away at the union. If all goes well and it is not too crowded, I settle into at a small corner table at Starbucks. I try my best to make the most of what have become sacred three-hour blocks of work time. I look forward to them. I plan in advance. And I strive to make the work sessions as productive as possible. So that, when Olivia asks me on the return walk to the car what I did at school, I can tell her: I responded to student projects; I worked on an article; I read. And, in return, Olivia will share the details of her school day.

Women's Ways presents much helpful advice, encouraging women in the field to seek out "stars" and star programs in graduate school, to find and build mentor/mentee relationships, to publish, be collegial, to stay true to and be good to yourself. As a parent of a young child, I couldn't help but notice how this advice reflects similar conversations Olivia and I have. We talk about what it means to be a student and the importance of modeling behavior after respected mentors/teachers. We talk about what it means to be fully present in class and about ways to be a good classmate to her peers. Our return walks across campus after her school day (and my power work sessions) often revolve around animated discussions of the new experiences of the day and how those moments leave her feeling good, not only about learning, but also about herself. In other words, I believe the suggestions Ballif, Davis, and Mountford offer are good practical advice for learners at any level.

Other moments of balance, I find, are less expected or routine than my campus walks with Olivia. My collaboration on this article is one such example. As someone in the fifth of her six-year probationary period as tenure-track faculty, my decision to devote time and scholarly attention to *Women's Ways of Making It*—a book that, as thought-provoking as it is, has no visible impact on my research agenda (no direct mention of writing assessment, qualitative research methodology or composition pedagogy) is both new and, I feel, a professional risk for me. After all, I could (or should?) allocate my energies to projects that more easily and deliberately identify with dominant scholarly conversations. Echoing the sentiments of the book, many established scholars would argue that mine was not the wisest tactical decision for any pre-tenure faculty to make, and yet I've found Ballif, Davis, and Mountford's study—in particular, of thinking through how I understand professional success in Composition and Rhetoric—has allowed me opportunities to connect with various colleagues and friends as we've chatted about their conceptions of success. It's in those moments of connection, whether with colleagues, friends, or on my walks with Olivia, that I find balance.

But, as the authors make clear, damaging professional, disciplinary imbalances continue to persist: powerful and destructive imbalances of power, access, expectation, opportunity, reward, and so on. For example, Ballif, Davis, and Mountford note that their survey findings focus on women who reported holding tenured or tenure-track positions, which they acknowledge represents only twenty percent of all women compositionists.

I suggest we build on the conversation *Women's Ways of Making It* skillfully introduces by turning our attention to better understanding how various other populations conceive of work-life balance, and how our colleagues—graduate students; part-time and full-time, non-tenure-track instructors; male as well as female colleagues variously positioned both within and beyond the academy—conceive of, aspire to, and feel constrained by perceived notions of professional success. There are many ways to make it, of course, of imagining, living, and understanding "it." For me, professional and, yes, personal fulfillment is bound to issues of locating and inhabiting a feeling of balance; however, it is we who go about the task of distributing our time, energy, and passions. I see our collective charge, then, as creating a disciplinary environment in which we feel more of a sense of control over the choices available to us, however we are positioned or identified. We need to be good to ourselves.

Making it as "Just an Adjunct": an "Other" Perspective
Deborah E. Morris

Like Lee, I see balance as complex and highly personal. As a teacher, researcher, student, and mom, my life is a complex intermingling of these seemingly diverse aspects of self; no single aspect fully represents who I am, and no position, title, or label fully defines me. So when I picked up *Women's Ways of Making It in Rhetoric and Composition,* I was both excited and expectant of what I would read in the text whose very title seemed to imply inclusivity within a diverse field. I read many helpful hints and interesting scholar profiles, but I didn't find myself represented within the pages. I realize I may not be the typical woman scholar as some conceive of her—after all, I embody multiple oft-ignored positions or perspectives, like adjunct, doctoral student, and mom—yet I was surprised as I read to find myself amongst those others, those beyond the scope of attention of the text; the text's clear and simplistic focus on tenure as the pinnacle of professional achievement in the field further frustrated me. Where was the complexity of identity (and, subsequently, of balance) that I, and many others like me, recognize in the ways that the various aspects of one's self connect, overlap, enrich, and sometimes seem to contradict each other in everyday life? I began to wonder, *why can't our field's notions of faculty success include scholar-mothers and long-term commitments to teaching and research in non-tenured or part-time positions? Does the tenure-only model truly represent our field in the twenty-first century?*

Though Ballif, Davis, and Mountford's text gives little attention to the largely female, non-tenured segment of the field's workforce, a group that Eileen E. Schell has likened to an "army of labor" (qtd. on 3), the NCTE does discuss disparities in the field in a recently revised position statement:

"[p]art-time and adjunct position are disproportionately occupied by women, who hold 39 percent of all faculty positions and 33 percent of full-time positions, but 47 percent of part-time positions" (sec. 1, par. 9). In a 2008 article, a college administrator suggests that colleges are responsible for creating structural imbalances (an idea later discussed by Mary P.): "colleges—champions of diversity—have created not only a two-tier system, but one in which adjuncts (who are likely to be female) are more likely to work longer hours for smaller paychecks than another group, tenured faculty members, who are likely to be male" (Jaschik, "Call to Arms"). Sadly, contingent faculty members (like myself) are often dismissed as being "just adjuncts" or "paraprofessionals" by those within the university, regardless of their educational training, scholarship, creative pedagogies, and dedication to their students and to their university community. And yet, NCTE recognizes that "part-time appointments represent positive options for flexibility in the academic career paths in higher education for many talented and highly qualified individuals" while also acknowledging "the incompatibility that some members of the academic community feel between the intense demands of the traditional tenure-track academic career and their family obligations" (sec. 1, par. 12). Interestingly, doctoral students now may be "rejecting the academic fast track" in favor of pursuing jobs at more "family friendly" campuses, according to a 2009 *Inside Higher Ed* piece. In order to have more flexibility and a better work-life balance, students are choosing careers at teaching-oriented colleges (Jaschik, "Rejecting"). This desired flexibility is found most often in non-tenure-track positions (as discussed later by Christine) or in adjunct positions (as discussed later in this section).

I realize that my personal and professional choices have not necessarily followed Ballif, Davis, and Mountford's suggestions for success. I chose to stay home with my children in the early 1990s when most women with degrees were heading into the workplace. I needed to be the one who encouraged their learning and imagining throughout the day, and I have precious memories of the joys and trials of mothering during those early years. When my children entered middle school and I was nearing age forty, I returned to school. I was the oldest student in all of my graduate classes and one of the few with children. I scheduled my classes around my children's school and extracurricular activities, and we often did homework around the dining room table with all three of us working on our respective coursework. I rarely got as much sleep as I would have liked, but the schedule worked for us. And during that time, I learned the value of mentoring. Throughout my MA studies, a strong woman scholar/researcher challenged me in the classroom and provided additional outside support and guidance. I still treasure Dr. Avon Crismore's encouraging words: "If you set your mind to it, you can accomplish anything!"

When I chose to pursue my PhD at an out-of-state school, a well-meaning graduate advisor said I couldn't possibly commute that far to complete my degree. I set out to prove him wrong. Moving wasn't an option, but neither would I settle for a program that didn't meet my academic needs. My chosen program was willing to work with me, and I have commuted for the past four years, usually taking only one course a semester. So, on one evening each week I have made the more than two-hour drive, participated in a three-hour seminar, and then driven home. In good weather, drive time and class time combined for a long, tiring day that often didn't end until midnight. This past spring I took two courses on back-to-back days, a schedule that required a hotel stay one night each week. Weather and road conditions still occasionally created other challenges, but the long academic road has had benefits, too, like being able to focus intensely within individual courses and being introduced to interesting new topics through interactions with several "waves" of beginning scholars.

As I enter the third year of my degree work, coursework is completed. I am preparing for preliminary exams and beginning the formal planning for my dissertation. My older son is a college junior and his younger brother began college this fall as a freshman. Life is changing, but the ability that made me something of a legend amongst family, friends, and peers—the ability to balance home, work, and school in wildly creative ways—remains. Time, after all, is a valuable commodity. As mother and scholar, I attempt organization, efficiency, and balance in all areas of life.

So, rather than teach out-of-state, I choose to teach several days a week at a community college near my home. As an adjunct instructor, I am paid only for contact hours in the classroom, yet I also maintain one or two office hours and interact with my student writers via e-mail throughout the week as well. I share an office with several dozen adjuncts from numerous departments, so I meet with students in the commons area, a space that is rarely quiet and often chaotic at best, but we make it work. Mentoring is also an important aspect of my teaching, especially with a diverse student population that includes many returning adult students, ESL/ELL/ENL students, and young single mothers. My investments of time and energy may not be reflected in my paycheck, but they are reflected in the successes of my students. And, I am keenly aware that I am choosing to make a positive difference at an institutional setting that many in academia might not see as at the epicenter of our disciplinary identity as writing scholars.

Interestingly, NCTE seems to understand that adjunct faculty "teach because they like to teach, because they want to make a contribution to the education of students, . . . and because they enjoy affiliation with our universities" (sec. 1, par. 11). Sadly, some university colleagues still fail to see non-tenure or adjunct positions as real jobs. In spite of this mindset, Maria Shine Stewart reminds that "[t]eaching without tenure is respectable work, even if it is not respected by all." I agree. I find joy in my teaching. I am excited about my studies and research. I am enjoying a new stage of parenting. My choices and my priorities as teacher, scholar, student, and mom reflect the complex intermingling of these aspects of self. And as an active member of a growing field that consists of gifted scholars within various academic settings and life stages, I wonder, isn't it time that we begin to recognize, support, and celebrate each others' choices—whether on or off the tenure-track? Perhaps "Women's Lives in the Profession Project," a newly-launched venture by the CCCC's subcommittee of the Committee on the Status of Women in the Profession will provide the necessary impetus for change within the field (see Conclusion for more about this project). After all, if we truly are to make-over academic lives, then we must encourage all scholars to live, learn, and teach from within those intermingling aspects of self that make us who we are and, ultimately, that allow us to "make it" in our own ways.

Making It in a "Different" Yet Ubiquitous Way: Non-Tenure Track
Christine Peters Cucciarre

In my copy of *Women's Ways of Making It in Rhetoric and Composition*, page three is full of scribbles and pen marks with large swooping circles all encompassed by one big box outlining the entire page. Although many of my annotations look similar, these are not my marks. This is the work of my three-year-old son. Although I felt guilty for leaving the book out and mildly irritated that he defaced one of my texts, the scrawlings reveal emotions that I felt often while reading this book.

Despite all the useful career advice this book provides, I finished it feeling a strange cocktail of shame and guilt. The undercurrent to the work of Ballif, Davis, and Mountford is that women who are successful in Rhetoric and Composition have to be published, well-known, and tenured. The text also recommends that women support one another and advocate for equal position, status, and pay. My current position subverts just about all of those things regarding women and the field of Rhetoric and Composition. My son's use of *Women's Ways* illustrates how I feel the text defaces the clear and justified choices women make when creating success for themselves in our field.

The book restricts the possibilities of being a successful academic in a number of ways. And if I believe those restrictions, I am woefully unsuccessful. First, the book left me out. I am in a non-tenure-track position. It is ironic that this book champions women as a minority in a field where we are hardly the minority, but yet "is in no way meant to ignore the number of women in non-tenure-track or non-tenured positions or part-time positions across the country who represent approximately 80 percent of those teaching writing" (Ballif, Davis, and Mountford 3). If eighty percent of women teaching writing are left out of the discussion, shouldn't the title of the text be *Less Than One Fourth of Women and Their Ways of Making It in Rhetoric and Composition*? Second, it shows how I've sabotaged our field. I am a continuing non-tenure-track (CNTT) faculty member at a doctoral-granting university. Although my position has parity with tenure-track positions in salary, benefits, and voting rights, I feel partially responsible for all that "we" are working against in a field that often struggles for respect by choosing to sign a non-tenure-track contract. Third, the book suggests that I've hurt women in our field because I am a woman who signed a non-tenure-track contract further undermining women in that already marginalized discipline of Rhetoric and Composition.

And yet, I am thankful that I have a job. So many of those I graduated with don't and won't as the economic situation continues to dim. Let's face it, many of us don't have a lot of employment opportunities to choose from. The options for recent graduates are meager and those of us who are employed cannot be faulted for, well, being happy about it. My teaching, my son, my field, my department, and my university all bring me much joy. But when I reflect on the situation critically, there are moments in my thinking, coupled with a visceral twinge in my gut that suggest I'm undermining the principles that are embedded in my hope for women and my hope for the field of Rhetoric and Composition. *Women's Ways* validates those unsettling feelings. Before reading it, I kept my non-tenure-track status on the down low. When people ask me if I'm tenure-track, I'll often avoid the question by saying, "I'll probably be promoted by my sixth year." When I read in the 2007 MLA and ADE report, "Education in the Balance," that "the concept of a non-tenure track faculty is an illegitimate exercise of institutional authority; it is, and it ought to be, contested by whatever means available," (15) my heart stiffens. The report softens the claim by saying that they recognize the trend's origins, but the report, nevertheless, makes me feel as if I've made some sort of Faustian deal. The MLA and ADE are certainly making their case for the equity and security of employment. But the truth is, the division is still hierarchical. The English department at my university promotes non-tenure equity even though I sometimes feel like an outsider during faculty meetings. The salary, the benefits, promotion, class choices, and almost all of the perks are equal with tenure-track positions. The biggest difference is that for continuing, non-tenure-track faculty, teaching comes first. Still, the university expects publication and professional activity in order to get promoted, but teaching is the main focus. Teaching college students is why I became a professor, so I like this arrangement. Yet, I know that research energizes my teaching, so I'm just as enthusiastic about my work outside of the classroom. I control the pace of my writing and publication; the deadlines are mine, not the university's. I can choose to put my students before my research and yet still easily intertwine the two.

I chose Composition and Rhetoric as a field for similar reasons. There's a practicality to the field that favors pedagogy, and an authenticity to the people in it, although many see those values as weaknesses. Gebhardt and Gebhardt say in *Academic Advancement in Composition Studies,* "Some in English studies continue to see Composition Studies faculty as a sort of fringe group engaged in practical—and so less worthy—efforts of scholarship and teaching" (8), another reason I often feel awkward in faculty meetings. I worry that in accepting my job I have forwarded the utilitarian nature of our field. For at least two decades, the literature has suggested that the constant battle of teaching and research will dissolve as the meaning of scholarship expands to include what we do in the classroom. And then there was, and continues to be, talk about universities moving away from the current culture of tenure, the kind of tenure Ballif, Davis, and Mountford seem to be sponsoring. These were all signs that the professoriate was moving away from the "publish or perish" ethos. Universities are indeed moving away from the current culture emphasizing researching and publishing, but the direction of the movement is questionable. My institution's current hiring rate is 3 to 1, non-tenure track to tenure track. The 2007 MLA-ADE report says that their survey of English departments across the United States shows that the ratio is even higher: 7 to 1 (9). Clearly, the divide is widening, not converging. According to the AAUP's report, "Tenure and Teaching-Intensive Appointments (2010)," "The tenure system was designed as a big tent, aiming to unite a faculty of tremendously diverse interests within a system of common professional values, standards, and mutual responsibilities." It also says that "By 2007, however, almost 70 percent of faculty members were employed off the tenure track." The MLA-ADE report confirms these numbers for English departments; it maintains that "only 32% of faculty members in English . . . hold tenured or tenure-track positions" (4). If we look at these numbers while considering sub-disciplines and gender, we know that in Rhetoric and Composition the percentages are probably even higher. A lot of us are not "making it."

Women's Ways of Making It doesn't represent this significant percentage of women teaching in the field. In fact, it represents and surveys very few. Of the 142 respondents, only 14 hold non-tenure-track appointments. Furthermore, when discussing balance and family, Ballif, Davis, and Mountford say, "we confront an irony: many of the women scholars in our study do not have children. And neither do we" (175). The back cover of their text says "this volume provides strategies for a newer generation of scholars entering the field and, in so doing, broadens the support base for women in the field by connecting them with a greater web of women in the profession." The greater web is very small. Ballif, Davis, and Mountford refer to Mason and Goulden's 2002 article, "Do Babies Matter?" and point out that "a full 62 percent of tenured women in the humanities and social sciences were without children, while only 39 percent of tenured men in the same disciplines were without children." But then Ballif, Davis, and Mountford note, "Importantly, the baby gap evaporates when women in non-tenure-track positions are included in the study. Women in these positions were more likely to have children" (180). This distinction is troublesome. The point Ballif, Davis, and Mountford seem to be making is that children and tenure are seemingly not compatible. But their highlight also suggests that non-tenure and children *are* compatible, further hinting that those whose main responsibility is to teach have it much easier than others.

When discussing *Women's Ways* with other women at a recent composition conference, several women admitted to me that they too grapple with these conflicts. They feel guilty and haven't openly discussed the consequences of their (our) decisions. It is time to stop feeling guilty and to vocally interrogate scholarship that fails to show the very wide spectrum of women who contribute to the field, even if those who write that scholarship are rarely in that wide spectrum. Perhaps we, in the field of Rhetoric and Composition, should stop looking at the old model of tenure and success and create some new category that is equally respected. We should choose to overwrite the book much in the way my son did on page three. His messy, but I'm sure satisfying, work illustrates the ambiguous nature of success and the many choices we all make to feel that sort of satisfaction. Especially in the current economic crisis, our critical outlook on our professional choices, our field, and our gender might be better used to promote the women in our discipline who "make it" by the thousands of students we teach and mentor each semester.

Making It Work: Balancing "Making Do" with "Making It"
Kim Hensley Owens

Like Christine and Mary P., I became a mother in graduate school, a development my mentors accepted and embraced. I did not, like Deborah, opt to stay home until my kids were mostly grown; my path is one in which mothering young children, teaching, and publishing coexist on the tenure track, and so, like Lee, I, too, perpetually seek balance. When I read *Women's Ways of Making It in Rhetoric and Composition,* I was in my second year on the tenure track, pregnant with my second child. While grateful for the profiles and advice offered in the book, I came away wanting more. I wanted more definitions of "making it" and more information about and acknowledgment of the lives of academics—particularly tenure-track academics—who are also newish mothers. At that time, with one child, teaching two or three classes a semester, and with a steady publication rate, more days than not I felt like I was making it. Other days were more like making do. Since adding my second child to the mix last year, "making do" days have outnumbered "making it" days, but I'm slowly figuring out how to make it again, and how "making do" can be all right, too.

To give readers a glimpse into my academic life as a mother, I offer a few verbal snapshots—moving chronologically from the job market to life as a faculty member. I can share these details, in part, because of the rising awareness and interest in the issues academic mothers face lately. Several *Chronicle of Higher Education* articles (see Gallagher and Trower; Kittelstrom; Wilson) and a number of books and edited collections have explored issues of motherhood and work (see Evans and Grant; Mason and Ekman; Podnieks and O'Reilly), publications that begin the conversation we extend here. I may not share Kittelstrom's opinion that we mothers should include the time spent growing, bearing, and nursing children on our vitas, but I do take to heart her point that this time is roughly equivalent to that spent researching and writing the typical academic book. Work-family researchers Robert Drago and Carol Colbeck have found that academic mothers try to avoid mother-bias by either attempting to "improve work performance at the expense of family commitments" or by trying to "hide or minimize family commitments to maintain the appearance of ideal worker performance." And yet neither of these bias-avoidance strategies seems to benefit academic mothers, academia, or the larger society, and neither works to alleviate the silences. We need institutional and systemic change to better integrate and support academic mothers, and with its large number of female faculty in positions of power, Rhetoric and Composition seems a particularly well-positioned field to begin to make that change. One way to move toward change is to share our choices and experiences. I hope by sharing some of mine, I can help make academic motherhood more doable for others. This is not to say I have it all figured out—I don't—but the more stories, experiences, and possibilities are out there, the better we can collectively work to make mothering and an academic career compatible enterprises.

I had my first child while writing my dissertation and went on the market while learning to care for my infant. I wrote job query letters with the baby on my lap, worked on writing samples while he napped, and filled out online applications while he grinned at me from a bouncy seat. But once I reached the interview stage, combining new motherhood with the job quest became more challenging. As Mary P. will describe, too, for a nursing mother campus visits present highly specific and infrequently discussed physical challenges. In my case, with visits scheduled somewhat abruptly—some with only a few days' notice—providing enough milk in advance became a fairly constant concern. I pumped whenever I could, often late into the night. I had to ask each search committee to arrange regular breaks and a private space for me to pump while on my visit—a request that obviously revealed my status as a mother, opening myself to possible mother-discrimination. I'm happy to report that most search committees were very accommodating of my needs as a nursing mother, which included a one-night stay, regularly scheduled breaks, and private spaces in which to pump.[2]

As part of my job acceptance, I thought I had negotiated a semester without teaching responsibilities when my second child came along—a sort of unofficial maternity leave via an alternate workload. But when the time came, fuzzy wording and a crashed economy had changed that scenario. Perhaps based on the experience of mothers at a few progressive research-extensive schools, there seems to be a perception that a semester release from teaching and an extra year on the tenure clock are typical in academia—they're not. One school I visited offers new mothers only two weeks of paid maternity leave. (While all new parents are permitted twelve weeks of *unpaid* leave through FMLA, few American families, particularly in this time of economic insecurity, can absorb three months with no paycheck: FMLA secures employment, but not solvency, during maternity leave.) With the help of a chair who is also a mother, in my first semester as a new-again mom I ended up teaching only one class, a graduate seminar. With course releases for administrative work and research, my workload wasn't "light," but it was flexible, and that was essential.

The following semester, I taught three classes plus had administrative responsibilities, but my chair arranged for two of those to be online classes. (Online courses on our campus are typically taught as an "overload" rather than "in-load" assignment.) The flexibility of that schedule enabled me to have only part-time daycare, with a few babysitters for semi-regular events like faculty meetings and PhD exams. This schedule allowed me to teach and write around my daughter's ever-changing nursing and sleeping schedule, and it almost made childcare affordable. I was lucky. In any economic climate, it may be impossible for universities to automatically provide teaching releases to all new mothers, but women should be made aware that they can arrange more-flexible schedules, and that these are best articulated in writing, rather than counting on individually negotiated, often tenuous, oral "deals."

Having children has forced me—or freed me—to focus super-intensely on work when I do have childcare. Most of my teaching, advising, research, and writing happens in those paid-for sessions, and in a few stolen moments during naps and *Sesame Street*. Sometimes I think about all the work I could complete, and how quickly I could complete it, if I didn't have quite so many family responsibilities; just as quickly, though, I realize how much life I would miss if I let work fill every moment of it (and we all know how easily academic work could). I also find that being needed by and allowing myself to focus on family at home means I work better when I am at work than if I hadn't taken that time. Being a mother, in other words, forces a life balance that in many ways benefits, rather than hinders, my work, insofar as I've had the flexibility to make that possible.

There are definitely days when I'm only making do. When I gave my talk at the 2009 Feminism(s) & Rhetoric(s) Conference, I had my then four-month-old baby with me. I had arranged for someone to hold the baby during my talk in another room; she hadn't shown up. But a sudden onset of separation anxiety would have made passing her off a challenge anyway. At the start of the session, my daughter was napping in a front carrier. We panelists agreed that I should speak first, in hopes she'd remain asleep. Alas, she awoke, wiggly, hungry, and angry, two minutes into my twenty-minute talk, so I gave my talk bouncing her in my arms. People in the audience didn't seem surprised—they even seemed sort of impressed. But for me it was not an impressive moment—I felt desperate. It was my third day of being at a conference with a baby; I'd rarely been more exhausted, and I was embarrassed. I knew my baby wanted to nurse, but I also knew I had a professional responsibility to deliver my paper. In retrospect I suppose that particular conference audience would not have had a hostile reaction had I nursed her then (that audience being quite unlike, say, that of the Australian Parliament when member Kirstie Marshall began to nurse her ten-day-old baby in session [see Bartlett 73-4]), but that solution didn't occur to me. The talk was neither my most confident moment as a scholar nor my happiest as a mother—definitely a "making do" moment.

After the session, though, a graduate student commented, "You make it look easy." I think I smiled and shrugged. What I could have done, at that moment, but didn't do, is shout, "IT. IS. NOT. EASY!"

And yet there are days when it seems like it is. A few weeks after that conference, I was at my home computer holding the baby while my then-three-year-old napped upstairs, alternating between writing and e-mailing feedback on a grad student's job materials. I asked him to overlook typos in my feedback because I had the baby in one arm; he wrote back that I should be a superhero in my own comic book. I basked in that comment: a "making it" moment.

There are days when I feel like I am most certainly making it. When I have a writing epiphany, when a student paper simply sings, when an article is accepted, when my son shouts out "That's your college!" as we drive by—those are glorious moments. As I enter my fourth year as an assistant professor, it's probably too soon to tell if those moments will add up to success by the standards Bailiff, Davis, and Mountford outline. But in my fifth year as a mother, I've decided there are three ways of thinking about my life on the tenure track with small children. There's "making it" as a scholar, there's "making do" as a scholar-teacher because I'm a mom, and then there's "making it work." And as long as I'm mothering and teaching and writing and publishing, I'm doing that, as the scholar-teacher-mother that I am.

Re-Structuring Possibilities
Mary P. Sheridan

Like the preceding authors as well as the academics Ballif, Davis, and Mountford interviewed, I too have been searching for the holy grail of balance, a balance that shifts as family and career responsibilities and opportunities shift. Throughout this re-balancing, I have faced a variety of options that reflect many of the choices faculty with children see for themselves. I had my first two (of three) children as a graduate student while at the University of Illinois at Urbana-Champaign. There, mentors like Gail Hawisher and Paul Prior modeled how senior colleagues can take a scholar/mother seriously as I worked to meet my scholarly and teaching obligations. My first tenure-track job showed the limits of that approach. Like many academic couples, my husband and I "split" our lives. I worked and lived with my children in one state while my husband worked and lived in a different state four days of each week. Many individuals at my R1 university were lovely, but the departmental culture was evident at a faculty welcome-back-to-school party; I was one of three out of perhaps fifty faculty who brought children. Ten years later, I am now a single parent going up for full professor at a Research Intensive university, a place far more hospitable to academics who publicly acknowledge they have families. Here, if I can meet the expectations of my job, which include attending some evening presentations and traveling for statewide conferences/professional meetings, etc., then it is not a problem if occasionally my children play in an empty classroom during my office hours or a faculty meeting. These diverging experiences reflect the successes and struggles that caregivers in academia regularly face. Yet, I believe that these seemingly individual experiences have a largely structural component. Therefore, in addition to examining how working parents make it in Composition Studies, as the previous essays explore, I would like to situate this elusive work-family balance in larger societal structures in which we in the academy are nestled.

First, it seems important to note that these struggles and successes are not unique to academia. In fact, nationally and internationally, there are high-profile conversations about work and family balance, and, as the cover story of the September 27, 2010 *Newsweek* makes clear, these conversations include, even privilege, a daddy perspective. As people and countries try to reconfigure what work and family mean in a globalized world where increasingly jobs are shifting, people are moving from familial support, and long-standing bread-winning gender roles are under intense pressure, it is clear that we need to re-think the work-family balance. Countries are experimenting with reshaping this balance, including offering more family-friendly policies so that men and women are offered the opportunity (and expected to take that opportunity) to have some financially supported time with their families at intense moments (e.g., birth or adoption; family emergencies; elder care). What is specific to the U.S., however, is how little we do to structurally foster this balance. For example, while industrialized countries like Sweden, Germany, Britain, Japan, and Australia have developed governmentally-backed family-friendly policies such as those surrounding paternity leave, "the U.S. is now the only wealthy country that doesn't bankroll a bonding period for either parent" (Romano and Dokoupil 46) after a child is brought into the family.

Without changing structures, it is hard to alter practices so that people can legitimately take advantage of family-friendly policies. And without this, people find work structures hostile to families. This finding is certainly the case in U.S. universities. "The Collaborative on Academic Careers in Higher Education" (COACHE) at the Harvard University Graduate School of Education notes that although both male and female humanities tenure-track faculty rate their working conditions positively as compared to faculty across campus, one area where the humanities rate in the bottom quartile is in the faculty assessment that their "Institution makes raising children and tenure-track compatible" (11). Struggles around this issue seem more acutely felt by women; of the few categories within the humanities that significantly diverge based on gender, women rated their "ability to balance between professional and personal time" as significantly lower than men did.[3] These findings echo similar recent reports that indicate that university structures and culture do not support women having children while in tenure-track jobs (see Kittelstrom; Mason).

There are always individual exceptions, yet looking at these trends in the aggregate highlights structural problems that for me, at least, require structural solutions. One solution is offered by Amy Kittelstrom, in the recent *Chronicle* piece, "The Academic-Motherhood Handicap": stop the silence around troubling university structures that cause individual women with children to make do, often to feel shunted to the second tier, in order to make it. Kittelstrom points out several layers of silence. One is the institutional silence that does not provide parents with (enough) information about the formal and informal policies surrounding parental leave. For example, a study conducted at Penn State University showed that in a seven year time frame, only seven of 500 eligible faculty took advantage of a formal parental leave policy, largely, the study authors argue, because the culture of this (and other) universities is that if you take that leave it will informally work against you at tenure time (Drago and Colbeck, qtd. in Ballif, Davis, and Mountford 177). A second silence surrounds employers asking good faith yet illegal questions (e.g., if potential employees have or plan to have children) in order to sell potential candidates on the great schools or the friendly neighborhoods. Now, job seekers may choose to relay personal information, as I felt forced to do when I went on campus interviews just eight weeks after delivering my second child; like Kim, I was still breastfeeding and needed time and privacy to pump. I was lucky to work with enlightened interview committees at schools like those at the University of Louisville and Colorado State University who found ways to accommodate my needs and still evaluate me on my academic credentials. Not everyone is so fortunate. A third silence is what Kittelstrom calls the "vita gap" due to pregnancy and bearing/rearing a child. There is no simple solution for tenure evaluation during this crunch of personal and professional timelines, but to do nothing is to ensure women who have children late during graduate school and/or on the tenure track will be at a disadvantage.

A second way to redress the imbalances in family-work concerns is for our professional organizations to be more involved in creating new structures. For example, the AAUP's "Statement of Principles on Family Responsibilities and Academic Work" offers this encouraging recommendation in its conclusion:

> Because institutional policies may be easier to change than institutional cultures, colleges and universities should monitor the actual use of their policies over time to guarantee that every faculty member—regardless of gender—has a genuine opportunity to benefit from policies encouraging the integration of work and family responsibilities. The goal of every institution should be to create an academic community in which all members are treated equitably, families are supported, and family-care concerns are regarded as legitimate and important.

Within our own field, CCCC provides resources for people to understand "Family Leave/Work Life Balance" as well as puts into practice family-friendly structures, such as providing day care at CCCC. These policy statements and institutional practices support parents as we try to find ways to make it.

With the help of such family-friendly structures, many of us are finding ways to create a balance we can live with. We are not superwomen or men, but rather people tactically working in the cracks, with progressive colleagues and/or thoughtful mentors who help us to develop workarounds that blunt the effects of current structural constraints. The previous narratives explain in very personal terms how people on the ground are reworking these structural obstacles in order to make it as scholars and mothers in Rhetoric and Composition.

Conclusion

We hope the narratives we put forward here suggest there is much we can do to build on the conversations *Women's Ways of Making It* introduces. By turning our attention to how various populations conceive of the work-life balance, and how our colleagues—graduate students; part-time and full-time non-tenure-track instructors; male as well as female colleagues variously positioned both within and beyond the academy—conceive of, aspire to, and feel constrained by the notion of "making it" in the common publish-or-perish model privileged in *Women's Ways*, we can better support each other in our endeavor to realize professional and personal fulfillment as mutually beneficial and sustainable realities. We have added a handful of new perspectives to the conversation, yet we are aware that there are many professional and life experiences not represented in our work. There are many ways to understand academic success. No one way can be the sole definition. We've shared our stories to spark additional conversations that can help us imagine, live, and make public this variety.

So what now? Where might we go from here? Our respective experiences have left each of us all the more aware of the importance of working together with our Rhetoric and Composition and department colleagues in order to establish more family-friendly academic structures that will benefit all of academia. First, we must address the seemingly individualistic idea of choice—the choice of caring for children, parents, family members—with the complex, often invisible structures that shape what choices are possible. Second, we need to expand the definition of scholarly success to include teaching, advising, and mentoring. Third, the profession must increase visibility of and a new acceptance for a greater range of balances, ones that promote various ways to be teachers, scholars, and family members.

To encourage this conversation and learn more about the rich diversity of women, their choices, and their work in the field of Rhetoric and Composition, the Women's Lives in the Profession subcommittee of the CCCC's Committee on the Status of Women in the Profession (CSWP) is currently inviting women within the field to narrate their own stories about working in this field (search "Start-up Kit," on the CCCC website). Family-friendly changes within institutional structures by our professional organizations can also encourage a greater range of balances. Among the recent moves toward family-friendly structures are: 1) CCCC now makes childcare available so that academic care providers need not choose one role over the other; 2) several professional publications work to make visible problematic issues facing academic parents, as is evident in this special issue and *The Chronicle*'s recent series of articles about the "handicap" of being a mother in the academy today. We applaud these encouraging steps, yet we call for more widespread dialogue and action.

Furthermore, introducing new policies or revising practices will benefit no one if those eligible do not take advantage of family-friendly structures. These structures must be reinforced as accepted practice, or they will be lost. We know this may not always be easy; the majority of those taking advantage of some policies are pre- or non-tenured faculty—a population who feels (and often is made to feel) powerless, vulnerable, and expendable. Therefore, we urge all faculty with families to take full advantage of current policies and to continue to speak up about unmet needs to colleagues and professional organizations (e.g., CCCC's Committee on the Status of Women in the Profession). And departments and established colleagues in our field must make family-friendliness a priority. Additionally, we need to respect alternative ways of being employed in the academy. Expanding our definitions of success is, in part, embracing all of our colleagues and their ideas regardless of status.

Clearly, experiencing professional success and fulfillment in a postsecondary academic context demands and should encourage a complex balance of the personal and the professional. This balance is more varied than many reports would imply, yet is more constricting than many of us would want. Broadening our understandings of making it will provide a long overdue revolution for the institutions and individuals within our departments, our schools, and more generally, academe.

Acknowledgements

The authors would like to thank all those who attended our CCCC roundtable discussion in Louisville and for the thoughtful comments attendees shared. We also thank Eileen Schell for encouraging us to continue the discussion beyond the conference. Finally, we would like to thank Jennifer Clary-Lemon, two anonymous reviewers, Melissa Ianetta, and Kevin Roozen for insightful feedback on various drafts of this article.

Notes

1 Although the descriptor "Research I" (R1) is no longer officially applicable, we use the term because it remains in regular use to describe universities with very high research-output expectations. The Carnegie Foundation for the Advancement of Teaching has revised its 1970 designations twice (in 2006 and again in 2010), shifting to a much more complex set of descriptors not yet in colloquial use. Carnegie's "new categories are not comparable to those previously used" ("Classification Description").
2 See "Pumping on the Market" (Owens), which offers advice to search committees and nursing mothers on the academic job market. An earlier version of this paragraph appears in that article.
3 The COACHE job satisfaction Survey, according to the Harvard study, included 1,114 respondents, with just under 54% female and just over 46 % male (37). The same survey focused on tenure-track faculty on the clock after one year in doctoral institutions.

Works Cited

American Association of University Professors. "Tenure and Teaching Intensive Appointments (2010)." Web. 27 Oct. 2010.

———. "Statement of Principles on Family Responsibilities and Academic Work" (Nov. 2001). Web. 15 Sept. 2010.

Ballif, Michelle, Diane Davis, and Roxanne Mountford. *Women's Ways of Making It in Rhetoric and Composition*. New York: Routledge, 2008. Print.

Bartlett, Alison. *Breastwork: Rethinking Breastfeeding*. Sydney: U of New South Wales P, 2005. Print.

Conference on College Composition and Communication. "Family Leave/Work Life Balance." Web. 27 Sept. 2010.

———. "Start-up Kit for Women's Lives in the Profession Project." Web. 27 Oct. 2010.

Carnegie Foundation for the Advancement of Teaching. "Classification Description." Web. 8 September 2010.

Drago, Robert, and Carol Colbeck. "Research at the Workplace: A Conversation about Family." *The Network News* 6.1 (2004): n. pag. Web. 6 June 2010.

Evans, Elrena, and Caroline Grant, eds. *Mama, Phd: Women Write About Motherhood and Academic Life*. New Brunswick: Rutgers UP, 2008. Print.

Gallagher, Anne, and Cathy A. Trower. "Figuring Out Flexibility." *The Chronicle of Higher Education*, 7 May 2009. Web. 10 Mar. 2010.

Gebhardt, Richard C., and Barbara Genelle Smith Gebhardt. *Academic Advancement in Composition Studies: Scholarship, Publication, Promotion, Tenure*. Mahwah: Lawrence Erlbaum, 1997. Print.

Harvard Graduate School of Education. "The Experience of Tenure-Track Faculty at Research Universities: Analysis of COACHE Survey Results by Academic Area and Gender." 2010. Web. 20 Sept. 2010.

Jaschik, Scott. "Call to Arms for Adjuncts . . . From an Administrator." *Inside Higher Ed*, 14 Oct. 2008. Web. 24 Oct. 2008.

———. "Rejecting the Academic Fast Track." *Inside Higher Ed*, 15 Jan. 2009. Web. 30 Jan. 2009.

Kittelstrom, Amy. "The Academic-Motherhood Handicap." *The Chronicle of Higher Education*, 12 Feb. 2010. Web. 10 Mar. 2010.

Mason, Mary Ann, and Eve Mason Ekman. *Mothers on the Fast Track: How a New Generation Can Balance Family and Careers*. Oxford: Oxford UP, 2007. Print.

Mason, Mary, Marc Goulden, and Nicholas H. Wolfinger. "Babies Matter: Pushing the Gender Equity Revolution Forward." *The Balancing Act: Gendered Perspectives in Faculty Roles and Work Lives*. Ed. Susan J. Bracken, Jeannie K. Allen, and Diane R. Dean. Virginia: Stylus, 2006. 9-30. Print.

Mason, Mary Ann. "Do Babies Matter?" *Academe* 90.6 (Nov. 2004): 10-15. Print.

Modern Language Association and The Association of Departments of English. "Education in the Balance: A Report on the Academinc Workforce in English" *Modern Language Association*. MLA, 2007. Web. 10 Dec. 2008.

National Council of Teachers of English. "Statement from the Conference on the Growing Use of Part-time and Adjunct Faculty." *NCTE Guideline*, 1998-2010. Web. 11 Aug. 2010.

Owens, Kim Hensley. "Pumping on the Market." *Inside Higher Ed*, 23 Aug. 2010.

Web. 8 Sept. 2010.

Podnieks, Elizabeth, and Andrea O'Reilly, eds. *Textual Mothers/Maternal Texts: Motherhood in Contemporary Women's Literatures.* Waterloo: Wilfrid Laurier P, 2010. Print.

Ad Hoc Committee on Staffing. "Education in the Balance: A Report on the Academic Workforce in English." Association of Departments of English, 10 Dec. 2008. Web. 30 Jan. 2008.

Romano, Andrew, and Tony Dokoupil. "Men's Lib." *Newsweek* 27 Sept. 2010: 42-49. Print.

Stewart, Maria Shine. "Adjunct Barbie." *Inside Higher Ed*, 6 Apr. 2010. Web. 7 May 2010.

Wilson, Robin. "How Babies Alter Careers for Academics." *The Chronicle of Higher Education,* 5 Dec. 2003. Web. 10 Mar. 2010.

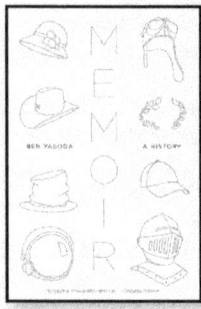   

BEN YAGODA
Memoir: A History
"Yagoda is one of the most subtle—and entertaining—writers about writing one can find. His history of the memoir reads between the lines—and the lies—with illuminating precision."—Ron Rosenbaum, author of *The Shakespeare Wars*.
Riverhead • 304 pp. • 978-1-59448-482-7 • $16.00

BETSY LERNER
The Forest for the Trees
An Editor's Advice to Writers
Revised and updated to address the dramatic changes that have reshaped the publishing industry in the past decade.
Riverhead • 304 pp. • 978-1-59448-483-4 • $16.00

ELIF SHAFAK
Black Milk: On Writing, Motherhood, and the Harem Within
Translated by Hande Zapsu
Viking • 288 pp. • 978-0-670-02264-9 • $25.95

PHILIP ZALESKI, editor
The Best Spiritual Writing 2011
Introduction by Billy Collins
Ranging from poetry to essay, this anthology contains work by some of the nation's most esteemed writers, including Rick Bass, Philip Yancey, Terry Teachout, Robert D. Kaplan, and others.
Penguin • 272 pp. • 978-0-14-311867-1 • $16.00

SHERRY ELLIS &
LAURIE LAMSON, editors
Now Write! Screenwriting
Screenwriting Exercises from Today's Best Writers and Teachers
Features never-before-published writing exercises from the acclaimed screenwriters of *Cape Fear*, *Raging Bull*, *Ali*, *Terminator 2*, *Fame*, *Groundhog Day*, "True Blood," and "The Shield."
Tarcher • 256 pp. • 978-1-58542-851-9 • $14.95

JORGE LUIS BORGES
On Writing
Edited with an Introduction and Notes by Suzanne Jill Levine
This selection of essays offers a comprehensive and balanced account of the evolution of Borges' thinking on the craft of writing.
Penguin Classics • 128 pp. • 978-0-14-310572-5 • $14.00

KERI SMITH
Mess
The Manual of Accidents and Mistakes
Perigee • 192 pp. • 978-0-399-53600-7 • $12.95

MARILYN ALLEN
& COLEEN O'SHEA
The Complete Idiot's Guide to Book Proposals and Query Letters
Alpha • 304 pp. • 978-1-61564-045-4 • $16.95

Penguin Group (USA)
Academic Marketing Department   375 Hudson St.   New York, NY 10014
www.penguin.com/academic

On (Not) Making It In Rhetoric and Composition

Robert Danberg

That a successful professional life in Rhetoric and Composition depends on a PhD, a tenure line, and an extensive publication record is complicated by the demands that family makes on a professional life. The notion of "making it" in Rhetoric and Composition can also complicate how the field judges the contributions of its participants and the variety of paths to success they take. The essay troubles the concept of "making it" by exploring how a "fatherhood," which looks in many ways like "motherhood," affects the way a practitioner who earns a PhD mid-career finds the authority to speak as a scholar, writer, and parent.

I expect I'm a familiar type in our field: someone who has come from a career in the writing classroom to Composition and Rhetoric as a research field. I am forty-five years old and I completed my PhD in Composition and Cultural Rhetoric in 2010. When I began PhD work, it was as if I'd begun again; I joked that for years I thought I'd been teaching writing and now I realized I was teaching composition. I thought I *had* been in the field. Acquiring the PhD put me simultaneously at the beginning of a career and the middle of a life, and, in a way particular to composition, in the beginning and middle of a career, where experienced teachers turn mid-career to PhD work. Though many factors have influenced my work life, I'd say the ones that affected me the most all stem from the way I chose to be a father.

Sondra Perl describes the changes children can bring to your professional and creative life when they pull you into their orbit, like an asteroid out of the sky. In a 1998 essay, "Composing a Pleasurable Life," she writes how, in the first part of her career, she resisted marriage and children to focus on a demanding, exciting professional life, although to call it demanding suggests that it was more than she wanted. It was, in fact, exactly what she wanted. The essay describes a woman who found a calling in a new field that combined much of what interested her, professionally and personally. She became a scholar, a teacher, a writer, a collaborator, and a creator. She taught full time, earned her doctorate, conducted important research, wrote, and traveled throughout New York City to work with and educate teachers. Her life was full of work in the way that work sometimes blesses us, times when, as Perl puts it, we have a sense of ourselves as someone with work to do in the world.

But when her daughter was a toddler, she and her husband Arthur had twins who, unlike their mild-tempered first child, didn't sleep. After a difficult, sleep-deprived time, she made a series of hard decisions.

> The first sane thing I do is resign as a director of the Writing Project. Then I request as simple a teaching schedule as possible. Then I stop presenting at national conferences. Then I stop attending local meetings. I have already stopped writing.
>
> As my professional world recedes, I am distraught. Losing the sense of myself as someone who has work in the world has been my greatest fear. Certainly I have been warned by women writers that children (more than one, Alice Walker cautions) will thwart creativity. Now, here I am, teaching, still, but only as a break from what I have strenuously avoided all my life and which now dominates my entire existence: two crying babies, one toddler, dirty diapers, piles of laundry, ear infections, antibiotics, Sesame Street, and hours of Dumbo. (Perl 249)

I recognized her distress when writing no longer seems viable and teaching, like writing, is no longer an exciting laboratory but more like work. Like she did, I fear losing "my sense of myself as someone who has work in the world."

I found Perl's essay when I looked for expressions of "making it" in Rhetoric and Composition that weren't tied to professional research and a tenure line. *Women's Ways of Making It in Rhetoric and Composition*, the 2008 book that's begun a lot of conversation over what it means to "make it" in the field, describes a vision of professional success many in Composition and Rhetoric aspire to. Its authors imagine women with tenure and a PhD, who publish well, who are "frequent keynote speakers," and who mentor other women in the field (Baillif, Davis, and Mountford 7). The authors' vision reminds me of the tangled expectations many of us find ourselves knotted up in. I find the description poignant because it expresses something more than success. It could count enough towards "making it" to be a tenured PhD with a serious publication record, but they also imagine women who influence the field and take up the task of mentoring others. It expresses a desire to recreate or change the past by being the mentor one never had. It expresses a desire not only to be heard, but to have fame.

The authors acknowledge that while many of the informants surveyed as part of their research concurred with the authors' initial expectations, some respondents challenged them. This make sense, since Composition and Rhetoric is a field made up of many, many different kinds of professional roles and participants; it could hardly be a field, or even a knowledge domain, if it relied solely on the contributions of tenured scholars. Besides, Rhetoric and Composition has always invited many kinds of wisdom into it, and the domain of Rhetoric and Composition is rich and complex because of the variety and number of contributions made to it.

Perl's essay appeared in an anthology published in 1998 entitled *Women/Writing/Teaching*. *Women/Writing/Teaching* mixes poets and fiction writers associated with composition and collects personal essays on what it means to be a woman called to write, as well as study and teach. Nancy Sommers, in her contribution to the anthology, sums up the complicated calling the volume describes. She writes,

> I want my students to know what writers know—to know something no researchers could ever find out, no matter how many times they pin my students to the table, no matter how many protocols they tape. I want my students to know how to bring their life and their writing together. (174)

The calling she describes puts this creative tension at the heart of the ethical, intellectual, and even spiritual project of writing and teaching writing.

> It is in the thrill of the pull between some else's authority and our own, between submission and independence, that we must discover how to define ourselves. In the uncertainty of that struggle, we have a chance to find the voice of our own authority, finding it, we can speak convincingly . . . at long last. (174)

Sommers calls this struggle a means to find a convincing voice we can speak through as we wrestle with submission and independence, or, in another sense, as we wrestle with aspirations and obligations. The tension between what we want and what we believe is our responsibility, between the authority we submit to and the creative reinterpretation that good work demands always troubles how we define who we are to try and speak at all.

A Jewish folktale explains the dilemma.

There was a prince who thought he was a crow.

He squatted under the table in his bedchamber, naked, with his hands tucked under his armpits to make "wings."

His doctors, the royal counselors, and his minders stood before his door consulting, as they had for several months, when an old man appeared at the castle gate and insisted he had a cure. He was led to the group outside the door who, at the end of a lengthy private consultation, agreed that something was better than nothing, and allowed the old man to examine the prince.

The old man entered the room.

The prince ignored him and pecked at the rug.

Then the old man took off his clothes and joined the prince under the table.

"What are you doing here?" the prince said.

"I am also a crow," answered the old man.

In the evening, he left.

This continued for the next several days.

Then, the old man brought in a tray.

"What are you doing?" the prince said.

"What do you think I'm doing," the old man said, "I'm having a piece of cake and a glass of tea. You can be a crow and eat cake and drink like a man."

The prince joined him.

And so it continued. Every few days the old man added something. The old man would say, "You can be a crow and wear pants like a man." Or, "You can play cards at the table like a man and still be a crow."

About two months later, the old man and the prince were playing Go Fish over dinner at the table, fully dressed.

"You know what the trick is," the old man said as he gave up a two.

"No," said the prince, who picked up the two.

"The trick," said the old man, "is never forgetting you're a crow."

When the story starts, I always wonder what it's like for a man to think he's a crow, and by the end, I am thinking about what it's like to be a crow who must pretend to be a man.

As a thought experiment, I wondered if my grandmother, Anne Sklov thought she'd "made it," and how my father knew he had.

Anne Sklov came from a Jewish immigrant working class family. She and my grandfather lived modestly in an apartment in Co-op City in the Bronx during most of my life. The only ostentatious thing they owned was a mirror with a thick gilt frame, twisted gold that held a four-by-four pane, which hung over the living room couch. At the mirror's base a button could be turned which changed the mirror to a "painting": a forest clearing surrounded by heavy-limbed trees and branches that hung down over the banks of a brook that ran over crags. My grandmother was fond of art, but not fond of Picasso—she'd seen an exhibit at the Museum of Modern Art and found it disturbing. She was a secretary and my grandfather was a bank examiner.

Something sticks with me from the visit I made when I dropped out of college and took a bus to San Diego, where she'd retired with my grandfather.

When I arrived in San Diego, the first thing she showed me in their small, rented apartment was a gas fireplace she could switch on and off. That weekend, she took me to Cabrilho Point and said, "Look, it's as pretty as a picture postcard," which meant that the blue water and blue sky and still boats were beautiful, and thus, true, and should be remembered.

Later, we sat in the laundry room, folding. She wasn't concerned about my future, only my happiness, so we talked very little about what the hell I was doing and folded the laundry. She showed me how to fold a fitted sheet, which I wish I could ask her about now.

The laundry room was cleaner and brighter than the one in Co-Op City, but more or less the same as laundry rooms and Laundromats everywhere. Stacked washers and driers, baskets on wheels, plastic benches and Formica-topped tables. She folded and folded, made the corners square, and imbued, as she always did when she folded laundry, each piece with the generosity she felt toward those who were part of her life, which was evident in the creases and corners of the folds, and in the neat stacks she made for each person.

I expect if I'd asked her if she had made it then, she might give me the same answer she gave me when I asked her what it was like to be a Jew in the forties: "I don't think it was like anything. It just was." But she saw to it that her life afforded her moments to appreciate beauty, and she had an aesthetic sense of time and her surroundings.

I remember my father once told me how he knew he'd made it once when he was twenty-one. He used to get a trim, a shave, and a manicure every week then—a manicure was a "guy who made it" thing in the fifties and early sixties. We went to LeWinter's Bungalow colony during the summers in 1969 and 1970. He owned a maroon Pontiac Bonneville with a white hardtop. He'd dropped out of high school, married my mother, and went to work as a stock boy for Shelburne Shirts. By the time he was twenty-one, he'd worked himself up to sales. Many years later when he became Vice President of Shelburne, he started smoking cigars and driving a silver Cadillac. He also began to wear hats, the kind of hats men his father's generation wore in movies until the fifties. I was nineteen or twenty then, and I remember wondering if the Cadillac and the cigars and the hats were, like the haircuts and manicures, a sign that he'd made it once again.

Since my father's life encompasses the height and end of the Jewish garment industry, his fortunes are tied up in its fortunes. Shelburne, my father's "place," closed when he was in his fifties. Small family-owned companies like it disappeared into other, larger entities. Manufacturing and management moved South, while manufacturing continued on to China, South America, and Pakistan. Just before Shelburne closed, I came home from college, about to graduate. I didn't know that he'd begun to negotiate an end to that part of his life or how worried he was about losing ground.

On my way out the door, I reeled off what I might want to "be"—an actor, a writer, a teacher, a rocket scientist, a G-man, an astronaut—and where I might live—Brooklyn, Portland, Seattle, Austin, Chicago (still suburbs of the hope to "make it" for graduates of artsy liberal arts colleges)—while my father sat in the corner of the couch looking at the TV in the opposite corner. Now I know that behind his wide forehead, the maps were spread out on the table and the flags were on the maps.

He said, "I don't know what to tell you. I didn't have those choices."

Last summer, I sat with him on the deck of his home in the "over fifty-five" community where he lives, quite comfortably, with my mother. He shared with me a detail from his childhood, which I knew had been hard.

We lived in a house of beds, he told me. The living room had a bed each for him and his three siblings. His parents took the bedroom.

"And we used to make toast over the open gas flame on the stove."

As another experiment, I replaced "rhetoric and composition" in the phrase "making it in rhetoric and composition" with "financial services," "dog walking," "raising children," and "love." I found it unproductive to say "making it as a parent" and awkward to say "making it in love," but productive to say "making it in dog walking" or "making it in stock trading." When I thought about "making it in love," the awkwardness of the phrase put me off—part bad slang, part bad self-help.

Dog walking and stock trading made sense though, since in each case success can be quantified: How many dogs; how many dollars? Does this dog walker want to be the boss of dog walkers and count her dogs in the teens or hundreds? Does this trader want to throw it all in and open a barbecue restaurant when she makes her first million? Will the trader know she's made it when she can throw it all in? Will the dog walker conclude that making it isn't worth it if "it" gets between her, the animals, and their owners?

"Making it as a parent" implies that one day I'll no longer worry whether my children are safe, say no to drugs, or choose mates wisely; or whether my homework support, clear limits, and R&B and Soul will guarantee good students, moderate eaters, and people I let work the car radio with impunity.

Still, the choice of how I would be a father has made the most difference when it came to "making it in rhetoric and composition" because once I decided how I would be a father, I spent most of my time "not making it in rhetoric and composition." I attended no conferences, I served on no graduate committees, I wrote no papers for publication.

We—my family—ground out the PhD life: teaching, exams, and the dissertation process; the commute, the weather, and the constant search for work to keep us afloat. No one with a family gets a PhD alone. My ex-wife had a demanding career and career aspirations, too. As a man, I've found I've had to explain how what might be described as the default position of mothering—to arrange play dates, fix dinner, pick up and drop off the kids, and be with them in all the everyday ways—was at the center of my life, and, as such, wasn't—how should I say it—one among many options to choose and perhaps set aside in favor of something else. I arranged my schedule to pick up my son from the bus at three and to take him to school or the bus stop. Sometimes my daughter stayed home with me. It was my contribution. I cooked meals and shopped and did a persistent but lousy job of housework. I learned something about mothering that added to the way I see fatherhood—placing me in relation to my children in a way that feels like I've taken an oath and a spell has been cast over me.

It is like a spell in that it is a mysterious, powerful experience in which I am compelled to act, suffer, and enjoy in ways that would baffle the person I was before my children were born. It's like an oath in that it feels like a promise that could not have been made any other way.

So, like they did for my mother, worries about my children distract me at work. On normal days, my daughter GoGo and I get home at 6 p.m., and if I haven't made dinners to freeze on Sunday, things get severe. I found a good after-school program for her but it costs an arm and a leg. Still, it's one less worry to know she's someplace she likes that I can trust, since it's crucial I show my department that I am *present*—can make the meeting, meet the visitor. And it's crucial, I've found in academia, to linger when the meeting is over. It's the academic's version of the businessmen's golf game, where deals are made between holes. It doesn't really always work to pack up quick because the commute is long and the weather wet.

In my career, I've had women as bosses most of the time—at least three quarters of my career—and I've been fortunate because I've found, almost uniformly, that employers have helped me find a way to juggle work, school, and family. It came at a cost, but I was able to work. Often, I took jobs so I could split days and nights when I was married and now that I am a single parent, sympathetic bosses have continued to help me to sort sick days, pick ups, and drop offs with class and work schedules.

I take heart from many of the women I've worked for and many of the women writers I've known whose careers followed the arc of their families. They found their way to work and grew more creative as they grew older and their children grew more independent. I also discovered that it helped not to see my life as having shrunk to something, but to go deeply into what it is right before me; I could find my art in it. But at work and in graduate school, it is simply true that to be taken seriously as a professional requires a certain kind of effort and commitment, and to "not be taken seriously" is the kiss of death. It certainly diminishes the likelihood that one will find opportunities where one can be taken seriously.

Still, despite the obstacles that women face in our profession, I was struck by how, in *Women's Ways of Making It in Rhetoric and Composition*, professional success offers the same satisfactions, makes the same demands, and takes the same toll on women that the garment industry took on my father. Like the professionals its authors hope to discover, he relied on mentors to help him navigate a world he brought native intelligence to, but little family experience to draw on. Like him, many successful women find it hard to "have a life" and also succeed beyond expectations; and the kind of professional success that he and those who "make it" enjoy requires single-mindedness, determination, and the support of others. The authors of *Women's Ways of Making It* ask their subjects how to "have a life" when professional success demands so much; but for these women, like my father, like Sandra Perl and Nancy Sommers, the work is the life they have. The difference between me and my father, of course, is that he could not have considered the choice to be the kind of father I have been. The difference between me and my mother is that I—and my ex-wife—regarded it as a choice.

Another feature of *Women's Ways of Making It in Rhetoric and Composition*, which may be attributed to the fact that it offers practical wisdom, is that it's possible to focus on the good advice it offers and overlook its other realities. In the last part of the book, which devotes single chapters to women whose careers model the kind of success the book's authors describe—Andrea Lunsford, Susan Jarratt, Jacqueline Jones Royster, and others—car accidents, unexpected divorce, rebellious children, professional setbacks, and untrustworthy colleagues eddy on the surface of career biographies intended to exemplify "making it." And by and large, the careers they recount, while successful, do not in general follow a straight path from college to graduate school to professional success. As a student of mine assured me once, "The long way draws sweat; the short way draws blood."

Another reason I find the vision of success the book describes poignant is because it reminds me of how tempting it is to believe that the effort I exerted to bring work, family, and ambition into line translated into anything other than a temporary solution to outcomes I might have been able to do little more than cross my fingers over. I don't know if a book in which men were offered as models of "making it" would allude to the subject's teenager's adjustment to moving following a divorce in the context of a new phase of his career; but in chapter after chapter in which exemplary women recounted the lives they have made for themselves in the field, in whirled a car wreck or a crisis at work. Stories told this way also describe someone who has made it; she is wise enough to admit uncertainty, embrace it, and make it part of the work itself. She also knows the difference between her work and the field.

We who teach Rhetoric and Composition find strength in the idea that understanding language is the key to understanding everything—which makes me wonder if potters think everything can be explained by the containers we put things in and how they are fashioned—and we are also prone to thinking that there is an "everything." We convert what surrounds us into texts. We believe that language and texts construct us—some in strong ways and others in weak ones—and if a text can construct an identity, changing the text can change *who comes next* or who we are right now.

Even as I embrace writing's transformative potential and mystery, a mystery worth spending my life with, I consider the belief that how we *understand* language and texts puts that mystery to rest. I call it "Balaam's fallacy." Balaam is the prophet in the Torah that King Balak hires to curse the Israelites camped across King Balak's land. Despite every effort to avoid doing so, every time Balaam opens his mouth to curse, he can only bless, eloquent, elaborate blessings that became part of daily liturgy. I've always seen Balaam as a kind of very-successful court magician: your neighbor's grass withers when he curses it.

He's definitely made it in his field.

However, Balaam believed that he had control over events because he has control over words. Instead, my life is not a text to read. It's more like a book I sit down to analyze that, every so often, someone snatches from my hand to throw under a bus, or takes from my hand to tell me I am loved, or I drop because I hear a thump and tears in the next room or tires squeal in the street.

Then, all at once language is no longer my instrument; I become an instrument upon which other powers play.

My son Rubin helps out some, but he's fourteen, and fourteen is like four: tall enough to scrabble a hand around in the knife drawer but not tall enough to see what's inside. When he calls me at work to say he and a few friends were going to hang out at home after school and have a snack, he perturbs the seismograph. Right now I know he means *Pardon the Interruption* and *Around the Horn*—ESPN on TV—and that there won't be any orange juice left for tomorrow morning, there will be dishes on top of the other dishes, and the lunch snacks will be gone. But—well, this doesn't make me different from my own mother or grandmother—I know that I'll need some combination of luck, hard work, and trust to keep him from driving into a ditch.

Lately, my nine-year-old daughter has taken to asking me from the back seat if I have what I want. I have lost several things—we both have—in the last few years, things we really liked. In the past, I've wanted lots, behaved as if I'd be satisfied when I had what I wanted, and, at the moment I did, often thought "I want this to go on forever" or "I wish I had someone to share this with" or "You know, a Cream Soda would make this perfect." Getting what I want seems to be a yellow light that tells me to speed up to beat the red. The desire to have a satisfying and challenging job, a rich and productive creative life, to be in demand professionally, and to be fully engaged in our family's life—there is great hope there, even while such a hope seems like a prescription for an "anti-anti-depressant," one designed to replace acceptance with a persistent feeling of dread.

I always answer that I have everything that I want—by which I mean that I am grateful that I have what I need. This sounds like a lie, or at least disingenuous. She knows I'd like to be able to afford a bigger apartment for us and her brother; I'd like to work closer to where I live; I'd like my visiting position to flip to a tenure line; I'd like to see one of the poetry manuscripts I've written between covers. I know that some of "making it" has depended on others—I write, others publish; I apply, others hire. What I want depends on what others give as well as effort, luck, and timing. I have to figure out how to persist, despite the likelihood that I will want more than I get and that my desires may run at cross purposes: I'll disappoint people I love and need to please people I don't like. If I appear disingenuous, it is because to say "Yes, I have everything that I want" is like not thinking of a peach tree while saying, "I am not thinking of a peach tree." Or saying, "I never get anything I want" or "I will stop wanting."

There's a Hasidic tale in which a wise man keeps a slip of paper in each pocket. One slip says, "The world was made for me," and the other says, "I am but dust and ashes." When he needs to find his way back from arrogance or despair, he reaches for the appropriate pocket. As I've considered my own choices in terms of "making it," it's occurred to me that either pocket works. It's not "in case of deep despair" on one side or "in case of arrogance" on the other. Both encourage a middle ground of gratitude, as well as an awareness of what is in my control. From this ground, I may find it possible to work with the arrogance that leads me to despair and the despair that sparks my angry arrogance. I think of arrogance and despair as two sides of a specific coin. Where it usually says "In God We Trust," these lines from Frank O'Hara's "Meditations in an Emergency" are inscribed: "I am the least difficult of men. All I want is boundless love." But in moments of dinner and dishes, papers to grade, and just before bed, remembering that I need to get GoGo a snack for her class tomorrow, to find cash to rent Rubin's cello, go to the Laundromat in the near future, write something I want to write and something I need to write, plan something I need to plan because that is my work and my job—if my daughter asks, "Do you have what you want?" I always can answer, without lying, "Yes," because at that moment I am in the midst of wanting what I have.

The trick, of course, is to remember I'm a crow.

Works Cited

Ballif, Michelle, Diane Davis, and Roxanne Mountford. *Women's Ways of Making It in Rhetoric and Composition*. New York: Routledge, 2008. Print.

Kinney, Kelly. "Of Queen Bees and Queendoms: Fairy Tales, Resilience, and *Women's Ways of Making It in Rhetoric and Composition*." *WPA: Writing Program Administration* 32.3 (Spring 2009): 150-54. Web. 13 Dec. 2010.

O'Hara, Frank. "Meditations in an Emergency." *Poetry* (Nov. 1954): n. pag. *Poetry Foundation*. Web. 10 Oct. 2010.

Perl, Sondra. "Composing a Pleasurable Life." *Women/Writing/Teaching*. Ed. Jan Zlotnick Schmidt. Albany: SUNY P, 1998. 239-54. Print.

Sommers, Nancy. "Between the Drafts." *Women/Writing/Teaching*. Ed. Jan Zlotnick Schmidt. Albany: SUNY P, 1998. 165-76. Print.

Narrating Our Lives: Retelling Mothering and Professional Work in Composition Studies

Loren Marquez

Responding to Michelle Ballif, Diane Davis, and Roxanne Mountford's *Women's Ways of Making It in Rhetoric and Composition*, this article provides a more expansive definition of "making it," and argues that not only should we focus on women who are professionals in Rhetoric and Composition at institutions other than the Research I schools and women who have already "made it," but we must look at the generation of upcoming teacher-scholars who are in the process of presently "making it"—women, young in their careers trying to obtain tenure, running writing programs, researching, teaching, mentoring, and mothering. This narrative expounds on how one junior writing program administrator on the tenure track at a teaching university with two young children sees her roles as mother and academic in Composition Studies as both complicated and complemented because each role sharpens the other.

On any given weekday morning, if you were to peek through my backdoor, you would find me in my kitchen, looking disheveled: hair pulled back into a makeshift ponytail bun, wearing one of my husband's old tee shirts and a pair of shorts, manically shifting from various kitchen appliances. My husband, a high school English teacher, is already gone by 7 a.m., and I am left playing the mother-multitasking game, "How Many Things Can I Do at Once?" While I wait for my son Nate's toast to pop up, I have filled the coffee maker, started to prepare my daughter Libby's bottles for daycare, and have gotten the jam and milk out of the fridge. Nate is asking, "Where's my milk?" and then demanding, "I want my milk!" while he turns his empty cup upside down, imagining that his fingers are a knight climbing up a tower. With coffee-starved frustration, I remind him, "Mama can't hear you when you don't ask politely." Libby is (at this moment) happily laughing at her brother and throwing her sippy cup on the floor and seeing how many times I will pick it up (which I dutifully do and rationalize it by counting this act as the squats I would do if I had time to exercise).

I grab the milk and all of Nate's lunch items, a sandwich, carrots, and applesauce, out of the fridge, and I ask him to write his name on the various plastic containers and bags with the permanent marker. He proudly and carefully makes the markings for his name while saying, "Vertical line, down-slant line, vertical line . . ." I get Libby's mashed peaches out of the fridge, grabbing a wet napkin because she always throws something on her, me, or the floor. (I have learned not to get dressed in my work clothes until the last moment before I walk out the door.) The toast has popped out and I give it to Nate with one hand and grab my coffee mug with the other. Nate happily plays with the jam, spreading it on his toast, and I fill my coffee cup and then sit down to feed Libby. She claps her hands when I say, "Peaches," repeating "p, p, p" as I make the "p" sound. She makes the "p" sound back. I take a sip of my coffee—finally.

In spite of the morning chaos, I think about how my children are experiencing the world through language: Nate writing his name; Libby associating the word with the thing itself and the sounds of the letters. The nights when Nate has homework, he sits at the dining room table with his fat pencil and writes a big "S" and little "s" on three-lined, triple-spaced worksheets and tells me, "Bookmark is a compound word." I think about how I am my children's first teacher. My children are experiencing the world and words through my everyday interactions with them. Their experiences with language bring a great deal of meaning to my daily life—I am sure because language and literacy are the focus of a great deal of my life—my career.

In the mornings, by the time the family is dressed, packed for the day, and in the car by 8:30 (I'm idealizing, it's more like 8:45), I feel oddly pleased with myself for all I have accomplished, so much so, that I feel like I should be clocking "out" for the day instead of "in." But as I pull out of the Pre-K and daycare parking lot after kisses, hugs, tears, and instructions to caregivers, I now must switch my mind from family tasks to all the professional tasks before me: send out manuscript, observe a TA's teaching, meet with a grad student about her thesis, prepare for my tenure meeting, put my course materials on my course Web site, meet with the Chair to discuss the advanced composition course, record grades, grade a stack of response papers, finalize lesson plans, and re-read articles/readings for the courses I teach. And that's only the "Academic Daily To-Do List."

Although many of us physically categorize the work we do in lists designated "work" and "home," and much of the work we do as professionals in academia is contained by designated spaces—teaching in the classroom or meeting students in our offices—the truth is that our lives as women professionals with children are not so neatly separated. Mentoring, nurturing, teaching, keeping the day-to-day world moving smoothly is all essential work, and work often not recognized for its value in both the home and academic spheres. As mother on the tenure track at a mid-sized teaching university, with two small children, I have come to see that our lives cannot be so neatly divided into separate spheres. My life as a mother has greatly infused my life in academia.

Michelle Ballif, Diane Davis, and Roxanne Mountford have begun to articulate the struggles of women in their roles as caretakers and professionals in Rhetoric and Composition in *Women's Ways of Making It in Rhetoric and*

Composition. The authors focus on desirable stages in a woman's career: how to become a professional, thriving as a professional, and having a life "too" within and beyond academic culture. Valuably, the authors also synthesize the major contributions to issues of gender inequality in the academy, notably how the tenure track timeline is not congruent biologically with a woman's reproductive timeline, and how administrative duties in WPA and writing center work often interfere with the scholarship productivity that is touted for tenure and promotion. Pointing to the works of Paula Caplan, Lilli S. Horning, Lindsay K. Kerber, the American Council on Education, and Theresa Enos, Louise Wetherbee Phelps, and Janet Emig, the authors cite the patriarchy of the academic culture, the lack of equality in the American university, the patriarchal dichotomies set-up by the tenure process such as research versus teaching, single-authored texts versus collaboratively-authored ones, and the fact that women are more likely than men to be the primary caretakers of children or aging parents—duties that often collide with the expectations of the academy.

Ballif, Davis, and Mountford's extensive literature review provides the foundation for the goal of their work: to provide "stories and strategies to help women obtain tenure track, succeed in tenure track and to balance career and personal endeavors" (2). As such, the authors define "making it" as women who "hold a PhD; are full professors at an academic institution; are tenured; are well-published; are cited regularly; have contributed a consummate piece in the field; are frequently keynote speakers at national conferences; are actively mentoring other women in the field; are able to have a real life, in addition to their scholarly activities" (7). And to illustrate women who have successfully navigated the gender inequalities of academia, or simply put, those who have already "made it," *Women's Ways* features profiles of nine *grande dames* of Composition Studies, those who were listed frequently on the authors' surveys as mentors or role models to many women in the field. These women include Patricia Bizzell, Sharon Crowley, Cheryl Glenn, Jacqueline Jones Royster, and Andrea Lunsford, to name a few.

And the profiles of these remarkable women are truly that remarkable. The honesty reflected in the accounts alone is refreshing for women in Rhetoric and Composition who, for example, face some similar struggles having a home life and raising children while attempting to thrive in their professions. Cheryl Glenn's account of going to graduate school as a necessary step to process the death of her brother and how she took one course at a time as not to disrupt her marriage and raising her daughter is defined by her statement: "Nobody goes to graduate school without sacrificing . . . everybody pays" (238). Similarly, Patricia Bizzell, who singularly instituted maternity leave at Holy Cross upon the adoption of her two daughters, frankly assesses the cultural norm that although men are more involved in childrearing than they were when she was in her twenties, issues of childrearing often "concern women in special ways because the culture addresses women in a special way" (210). And, like many mothers, Bizzell admits that working full time and having kids has been "very, very vex[ing] for me . . . . But I don't know that I could have done it differently . . . ." (210). Glenn and Bizzell, no matter how brilliant and productive, and resonant, do not, however, represent those professional women in Rhetoric and Composition who have chosen to have "early babies." Using research from Mary Anne Mason and Marc Goulden's longitudinal study, "Do Babies Matter?," Ballif, Davis, and Mountford claim that there is a large achievement gap between women and men who have "early babies," or babies born prior to "five years after his or her parent completes the PhD" (179). Men seemingly benefit from "early babies," whereas, women are at a strong disadvantage; therefore, women on the tenure track often avoid having children (180). In fact, the authors admit in chapter seven, "Creating a Life Within/Beyond Work," the irony that "many of the women scholars in our study do not have children. And neither do we" (175). And of the esteemed women profiled, only Jacqueline Jones Royster had a child while on the tenure clock, but again, Royster's case is unusual because she had been "promoted to associate and had more than enough publications to be tenured at Spellman College" (177).

Although *Women's Ways* is a valuable resource and profile of women in the field, and ultimately achieves the authors' purpose, as Halina Adams and Melissa Ianetta recognize in their review, *Women's Ways* is limiting in that it primarily focuses on women at research-oriented universities and the tenure expectations which correlate with a Research I university. The reviewers note that a "more expansive definition of 'making it'" and the category of women "might . . . [be] opened [up] further" (146). I would argue to open this definition up even further: not only must we focus on women who are professionals in Rhetoric and Composition at institutions other than the Research I schools and women who have already "made it," but we must look at the generation of upcoming teacher-scholars who are in the process of presently "making it"—women, young in their careers trying to obtain tenure, running writing programs, researching, teaching, mentoring, and mothering. This is a narrative that is growing more common in the field, as many women at teaching universities or with heavy writing administrative responsibilities are choosing to have children while on the tenure track.

As women in Composition Studies who work, give, write, parent, listen, mentor, read, present, teach, publish, administer, guide, evaluate, and who are of different cultural, ethnic, and economic backgrounds, different sexual orientations, and teach at two-year, four-year, teaching, and research universities, public and private, and who care for children, parents, or loved-ones, we need to write about *our* ways of making it in the field to provide a broader account and fuller definition of making it. The myth of the work-home divide needs to be re-imagined in our narratives and scholarship, not as a dichotomy, but as a system of reciprocal relationships that create both complexity and value in the lives of women professionals in Composition Studies and subtly subvert the patriarchal structure of the academy.

As a tenure track, Director of First-Year Writing, and Mentor to Graduate Students at a four-year, state, teaching university, and mother of two children (one of whom is an "early baby"), my professional life certainly does not put me in the same class as Andrea Lunsford. But what my account does offer in many respects is a valuable and equally admirable view of how one woman's work in her field and in her home life enrich each other—how mothering illuminates our roles as teachers, scholars, and mentors. And in these roles we can strengthen our students as they strengthen us—much like iron sharpening iron.

I define my own entrance into the field not by my first day of graduate school or the completion of my qualifying exams, but as a mother of a six-month-old son, a pre-professional actively on the job market, a graduate student in her last year of graduate school who was researching and writing about the effect of students' literate and performative practices on their academic writing, and an instructor teaching two classes to cover her tuition for registered dissertation hours. My husband, Paul, a high school English teacher at a private high school, secured the "steady job" for our family which allowed me to focus on graduate school full time. Before my son was born, my days were occupied with academic work, either research and writing or teaching. Now I often long for the days when I would sit at Starbucks for uninterrupted hours, sipping my three-dollar mocha, reading Platonic dialogues from *The Rhetorical Tradition,* studying for my qualifying exams in sweet solitude. After my son was born, I could not so easily fill my days with the ancients; the present condition of mothering filled them for me. I taught my classes in the evening, so that my husband could watch Nate when he got off from work. We tag-team-parented: he taught, then parented; I parented, then taught; and that was the routine established by the regimented schedule of the primary bread-winner and the flexible schedule of academia. For me, teaching part time in the evenings fit securely in the nook of our family life. The research and writing of my dissertation and securing a job did not.

In one corner of our tiny apartment, which up until the job search had served as the dining area, I had a chart with due dates for application materials, various folders with CVs, teaching portfolios, writing samples, and descriptions of each school and job for which I was applying. I had another desk in Nate's bedroom with a computer and Internet access to send materials to schools via online dossier services, and when I found two or three hours (at night, if I had a babysitter or on a weekend when my husband could watch Nate for extended periods of time) to write my dissertation. And in the middle of the living room, we had what I affectionately call the "baby corral"—a six-sectioned plastic gate that made a hexagon and ideally kept the baby from crawling into our kitchen cabinets (this was Nate's favorite destination). I fashioned the hexagon next to the couch, put in some of Nate's staples: blocks, books, and measuring cups (another favorite) and smiled satisfactorily as I sat him inside—I had just bought myself at least a half an hour of work time. I positioned myself on the couch, my laptop with me and began to proofread the methodology section of my study, with the eager sense of *needing* to get work done. I also wanted and *needed* to give my son the time, love, and attention that he deserved.

My plan succeeded—for about five minutes. I would sit on the couch and look at little Nate as he threw blocks, but then he would stare at me, with his big, brown soulful eyes. Then, the staring would escalate into pouty lips and then turn into lifting his arms and saying, "mama." I would answer, "Nate." Then, he would reply with crescendoed "mamas," then all-out tears and screaming—all in the course of about a minute! I opened up one part of the gate to include the couch so that there was no longer a physical barrier between Nate and me. I would pick him up periodically—every minute or so—and redirect him to another toy, but he still wanted more of me, my physical presence, next to him. He cried so much that I ended up inside the baby corral with my laptop to my right side, and Nate and blocks, and books, and balls to my left, and I oscillated back and forth between the two. This picture is representative of being a mother with small children in academia: oscillating back-and-forth between academic work and your children's needs, problem-solving, multitasking, and in the end, realizing that this is the reality in which you must accomplish your work. Our apartment was a spatial representation of the symbiotic nature of family, motherhood, and academia for me. There were no boundaries where I could exist without my son or he without me. There were no boundaries where my academic work could not permeate. Motherhood interrupted my work in academia, but it also showed me how to incorporate the roles of student and a scholar into my role as a mother. In the process, the roles infused one another.

I completed my dissertation, applied for jobs, graded papers, and planned my classes in stolen moments at night when Nate was asleep, or when I could arrange childcare, which was difficult because our family was 1,200 miles away; my support system, other graduate students, were dutifully working on their dissertations and teaching, and many of the reputable daycare centers would not care for children on a part-time basis. Time was my muse, my inspiration. And if she gifted me twenty minutes or two hours, I knew I had to use her well.

But, I also learned how to work in integrated moments—much like the one described—where I had to write alongside my son. I would place him on the Boppy breast-feeding pillow, nursing him while I proofread or rethought the organization of my methodology chapter. The myth of the solitary writer and thinker waiting for the muse to visit was just that: a myth. My son and I were symbiotic. There was no work-home divide. I was at home. I was sustaining him, and I was sustaining myself intellectually. I had never been so tired. I had never been so motivated.

This narrative of having a child during the end stages of graduate school is discussed in Ballif, Davis, and Mountford's work and reveals a more recent trend for women who choose to have children "when [they] are studying for comprehensive exams or writing a dissertation and teaching" (179) rather than to wait to have children during the tenure track or after they have achieved tenure. One respondent who had a baby during the end stages of graduate school remarked, "No one cares if it takes you five or seven years to finish, but they *do* care if you take a hiatus after graduating instead of going on the market" (179). Though there is much discussion of how the academy's patriarchal structure of the tenure track is incongruent with a woman's ideal reproductive years, my focus here is not to claim that women could, should, and have to "do it all." What I have found as a woman on the tenure track with two small children, both in my own life and in the lives of my students that I have mentored, is that the fallout from the patriarchal structure of the tenure track and the notion that one must first achieve success along the timeline most beneficial to men—often at the expense of women's ideal reproductive years—is manifested in a very real fear and anxiety. As a graduate student, my roles were not as complex because my responsibilities to the university were defined by my "student" and "graduate instructor" roles. When I entered the academy as a tenure-track Writing Program Administrator, mentor, teacher, and researcher, I more fully understood how these roles—and how motherhood infused them—were important in building alternative histories of achieving success in the field.

Two years ago, in an introductory writing course I was teaching, I assigned Adrienne Rich's "'When We Dead Awaken': Writing as Revision" at the end of the semester as a culminating reading before students revised their final drafts for their writing portfolios. I asked students to define revision as looking back and re-seeing their writing. I asked them to consider the time and work and language constraints under which they had produced their texts for the portfolio and to write a cover letter explaining how their writing had evolved. To frame one of our discussions on revision, I asked students to apply these same questions to Rich's work: How did Rich look back at her writing to see how it had changed over time? What work constraints of time or family did she work under? What language barriers existed for her?

During our discussion, however, students did not want to discuss the evolution in Rich's writing; they wanted to critique Rich's comments on motherhood and called her a "bad mother." They responded with either apathetic nods when I brought up patriarchal constraints or historical misunderstandings of women's plight for equal rights in the 1970s as "the olden times," as if it were medieval Europe. They struggled with a genuine sense of confusion about how a literary canon defines a discipline and how the male voice was the dominant model—even for female writers.

"Why couldn't she be a poet and a mother?"

"I don't think that women now experience inequality like women in the olden times."

"Why didn't she just write like she wanted? She didn't have to write like a man."

These comments, though disturbing, demonstrate how students grappled with the complexities of what it means for a woman to write in academia and to even be inspired to write in the context of patriarchal intuitions. They also represent the disparate positions that I negotiated as a feminist, mother, and academic while my students and I discussed Rich's work.

Rich's essay resonates differently with me now then it did when I was a student in my early twenties and before I became a mother in my late twenties, because I now recognize the constraints of academia and how those constraints restrict and often dichotomize the roles of mother and professional. Rich's rereading of Virginia Woolf's *A Room of One's Own,* illuminates the patriarchy that looms over Woolf as she writes, recognizing: "the sense of effort, the pains taken, the dogged tentativeness in the tone of the essay" (20). The same way Rich senses Woolf's constraints are the same way I now recognize the efforts of other women and mothers in academia. I know that it is not a small feat to write an article or to plan classes because time for a mother is painstakingly accounted for by demands of both work and home: by mentoring, by writing letters of recommendation, by supervising teaching, by conferencing, by editing and giving feedback, by children's class projects, washing bottles, shuttling kids to after school activities, making sure they are doing their homework, and the daily care of dressing, feeding, and the other work of caretaking. Rich's words and work recall for me the parallel between the invisible nature of "woman's work" and the invisible nature of women's administrative and service roles in academia. All of this work in both roles is expected and often doggedly attended to, while simultaneously unacknowledged.

And though my students pitted the traditional role of "mother" (often their own mothers) against Rich's negotiation of the complexities and constraints of being a writer and woman, I couldn't help but align myself with her text. For I related to Rich's accurate assessment of the lack of headspace and everyday activities that revolve around raising small children: "to be maternal with small children all day in the old way . . . requires a putting aside of that imaginative activity" (23) with a magnitude that I certainly could not expect from most of my eighteen-year-old traditional students.

I responded to many of the students' comments and questions with more questions, hoping to get them to consider alternate viewpoints: What are the typical texts/novels/works that you read in high school? Who wrote them? Do you know what the Literary Canon is? Do you think that women should have to choose between being mothers and writers? Who are the primary caretakers of the home and children?

I was running out of dialectical questions to push their thinking further, experiences to buttress Rich's points; and the historical context I was providing did nothing to clear up the general malaise of anti-feminism that was now hanging over the room. So I told them a little about my own plight to earn my PhD while raising a small child and teaching. "A woman who takes care of a small child is defined by time. You have to constantly feed, change, put down for a nap, wash bottles, while trying to free up the headspace to actually say something coherent. It's really difficult to be the source of life for someone, and a source of imagination and intelligence." And then not so eloquently, but realistically, "Maybe Rich needed to do something more intellectual than wipe her child's bottom."

Though that last comment garnered a few laughs (and a few looks of disgust), I had given them a real life example from my own life and not the perceived "olden times" that perhaps helped them to imagine the scenario a little more easily. And though I acted cavalier in front of my students while telling them the difficulties of negotiating writing a dissertation and being a new mother, I was keenly aware of the risk I was taking as I, their teacher, stood there before them vulnerably professing motherhood. Would my students see me as less of an academic now that they knew more about managing my daily life as a mother? Would they want to relate to me as a sister or mother figure? Would they consider me a "bad mother" who chose a career over staying at home full time?

And then a contemplative and soft-spoken young woman named Sam in the front row on the far right side of the room spoke. "I don't agree with most of you," she said as she looked around the classroom. "These are our mothers. These are our grandmothers. This wasn't that long ago."

Sam's comment has always resonated with me. In turn for sharing my experiences as a mother in the context of teaching, she gave the most poignant analogy, a relational one. Her comment helped me to understand that being a mother and being an academic do not have to compete or be separate from one another. These roles inform one another. They are relational. In the context of my class, as a mother and academic reading this piece, "'When We Dead Awaken,'" one of my female students taught me how to reread my role as their teacher and explore how my relationships are enriched when these roles meet or collide. Defining Rich's plight using a relational analogy, "these [are] our mothers and grandmothers," instead of a dichotomy between traditional and non-traditional roles of women,

Narrating Our Lives 81

allows for an alternate view of women in academia, women whose lives are infused by their roles as mothers and/or caretakers, teachers, and mentors. And in these roles we can interact with our female students as iron sharpening iron.

Yet, like our parental roles, our roles within academia as mentors, teachers, and administrators—adjudicating plagiarism cases, filling out paperwork, e-mailing the teachers we supervise, taking impromptu meetings, putting out small and large fires, chairing committees—occur within the context of relationships, relationships with our students, our children, our discipline, our curriculum, our departments, and our profession at large. Rich recognizes the privileged status of women in academia. But she also recognizes that the establishment itself is built upon the traditions of men. She calls us to redefine our creative energy in ways that draw on and unite these relationships (24). As a mentor to graduate student teachers in the English department, women often share their desires with me to be go on for a PhD or other professional role, but are hesitant to break the prescribed boundaries of academia. In the recent Fall semester, two of the ten women graduate students have come to me expressing concern that they are afraid to get pregnant—even though they want children—because they don't want to lose their funding for their TA-ship.

As their teaching mentor who has also had a child during graduate school, I explained to them that I would support their decision to have a child and also reassured them that I know how and will help them to navigate the administrative processes so that they are able to take leave. But what resonates most poignantly with them is the story of my experience and knowing that someone else chose to have a baby at a time academia perceives as less than ideal.

I tell them that I had a good model and mentor who supported my decision to have a child when I was in graduate school. My mentor, Carrie Leverenz, who, when I told her I was pregnant both celebrated and problem-solved with me, advised me how I could fulfill my requirements as her Assistant WPA from home while I took time off in late March one Spring semester to have and care for Nate. Leverenz understood my experience; she had a son while in graduate school at Ohio State and has since written about how women in mentorship roles in academia need to create a support system for women graduate students who choose to have a child. In "Mother, May I Mentor," Leverenz, Catherine Gabor, and Stacia Dunn Neely share stories of their support (and lack of support) when they were pregnant in graduate school or during their first years as professors. Leverenz's story is particularly poignant because she expresses her worry that having a child would affect her scholarship. But it is her mentor (Andrea Lunsford, no less!) who encourages her to write about "managing babies and academic life because so little had been written about it" (101). Leverenz acknowledges that Lunsford first helped her to recognize that "personal experience and intellectual work ought to be connected" and this connection has not only shaped "her scholarly career" but also her "mentoring of other women who long for that connection" (101).

This legacy of mothering and mentorship is one that creates empathy, support, and a visible picture of encouragement for those women who seek out our help when they are unsure how to make it as a professional and as a mother. By telling this story to my graduate students, who were troubled over the decision to have a baby during graduate school, I gained understanding of mentoring women who want to resist the binaries of motherhood and academia.

And yet, not only do our multiple roles affect our students in overt ways, but in our relationships with students, particularly young women who seek our mentorship, we give them a picture of not having to choose between being a mother and being an academic. One of my undergraduate students, Suzanne, who had been an exceptional writer in my advanced composition, decided to pursue her Master's Degree in English at my institution and was under my direction as a teacher in our First-Year Writing Program. I taught Suzanne for three years and worked closely with her as her Thesis Director, and she was also my Editorial Assistant for the university writing manual that the First-Year Writing Program publishes yearly. We formed a great relationship based on writing and respect. Upon her graduation, Suzanne wrote a letter to me which expressed her gratitude for my mentorship and encouragement in her writing and scholarly research. But what she remarked had most deeply affected her was that I had shown her what a working mom and academic could look like. That is what left a lasting impression on her. "I hope that one day I can be like you," she wrote.

When I first received the letter I was touched in one regard, but one part of me felt like a phony. *Be like me? I'm barely making it. All I want is eight hours of uninterrupted sleep.* But when I pull out this letter from my office desk drawer on occasions when I don't think that what I do is making a difference, or have had a really difficult teaching day, I realize that my life as a mom *and* an academic is visible and has given Suzanne a picture of making it. It has encouraged her that she can, if she chooses, do the same. As a teacher and a mentor, especially with Sam, Suzanne, and other young women in academia, I have forged relationships that strengthen these women but also strengthen me.

Writing about these moments where work and home life blur exposes the contexts and constraints under which women enter the academy, produce writing, teach, and interact with their children, loved ones, and their students; it also lets us participate in this transformation. Susan Jarratt argues that when we "define our professional activities in ways that include efforts to transform the world" we are practicing feminist pedagogy (115-6). My relationship with my son has always been influenced by my relationship to my work in Composition Studies, and now, even at a young age, he sees me going to work, typing, reading, and grading, and he recognizes the importance of literate practices in our daily life. He asks me to read to him, to write speeches and stories (because that is what rhetoric is and what Mama does!), or to make a newspaper that tells what he does at school. On the days when it seems like I am sacrificing time with him to go to work, I do know that by enriching my life, I have enriched his.

As a group of women professionals in Composition Studies, in the broadest sense of the term, we need to write about our home and work lives and the conditions under which we flourish in both of those roles in order to provide a broader account of succeeding or "making it." Consequently, when we tell and write our stories, we are creating an alternate rhetorical history of women professionals in our field, and by extension, we complicate and deconstruct the often patriarchal construction of professionalization. Occupying roles as mothers and professionals allows us to be better, more accessible role models for our students, especially our young female students.

Now, as I write this article my daughter Libby is inside the baby corral. (She is more easy-going than my son was and is content with just my presence.) But I am still doing the same thing, oscillating back-and-forth between being a mother and being an academic. I've come to see that the space that exists in this back-and-forth movement is generative. My mothering informs my teaching and professional interactions. It makes me become a better mentor to my students. My profession makes me reflect on how my children's lives are being enriched by having a mother who is not only committed to the education of her children, but also committed to the education of her students.

Libby is pushing the buttons on her Sesame Street Elmo Laptop. She presses a button, and hears Elmo say, "Four, Elmo sees four butterflies." She looks at me, delighted with her nearly-toothless grin. "Yay, Libby," I say. I clap my hands. She claps, too, proud of herself. I am proud of her, and I know she is proud of me. She is typing like Mama. She kicks her tiny feet in excitement and presses another button, then applauds herself again. In this shared moment, I know that my profession, my writing, my interactions with her, will forever shape her, as I hope I will shape the women who I teach, mentor, and guide, as they do for me.

Works Cited:

Adams, Halina, and Melissa Ianetta. Rev. of *Women's Ways of Making It in Rhetoric and Composition Studies,* by Michelle Ballif, Diane Davis, and Roxanne Mountford. *Composition Studies* 36.2 (Fall 2008): 144-7. Web. 9 Sept. 2010.

Ballif, Michelle, Diane Davis, and Roxanne Mountford. *Women's Ways of Making It in Rhetoric and Composition.* New York: Routledge: 2008. Print.

Gabor, Catherine, Stacia Dunn Neeley, and Carrie Shively Leverenz. "'Mentor, May I Mother?'" *Stories of Mentoring: Theory and Practice.* Ed. Michelle F. Eble and Lynee Lewis Gaillet. West Lafayette: Parlor, 2008. 98-112. Print.

Jarratt, Susan C. "Feminist Pedagogy." *A Guide to Composition Pedagogies.* Ed. Gary Tate, Amy Rupiper, and Kirk Schick. Oxford: Oxford UP, 2001. 113-31. Print.

Rich, Adrienne. "'When We Dead Awaken:' Writing as Revision." *College English* 34.1 (Oct. 1972): 18-30. Print.

MLA's essential standard guide for graduate students, scholars, and professional writers

"This third edition of the manual is indispensable. ... Essential." —*Choice*

MLA Style Manual and Guide to Scholarly Publishing
3rd edition

xxiv & 336 pp.
Cloth ISBN 978-0-87352-297-7 $32.50

LARGE-PRINT EDITION
Paper ISBN 978-0-87352-298-4 $37.50

Join the MLA and receive 20% discount.

Reorganized and revised, the third edition of the *MLA Style Manual* offers complete, up-to-date guidance on writing scholarly texts, documenting research sources, submitting manuscripts to publishers, and dealing with legal issues surrounding publication.

The third edition includes

- a significant revision of MLA documentation style
- simplified citation formats for electronic sources
- detailed advice on the review process used by scholarly journals and presses
- guidelines on preparing electronic files
- discussion of the electronic submission of a dissertation
- a fully updated chapter on copyright, fair use, contracts, and other legal issues
- a foreword by Domna C. Stanton on the current state of scholarly publishing
- a preface by David G. Nicholls on what is new in this edition

Modern Language Association **MLA**

Phone orders 646 576-5161 ▪ Fax 646 576-5160 ▪ www.mla.org

Course Design

Reimagining "English 1311: Expository English Composition" as "Introduction to Rhetoric and Writing Studies"

Todd Ruecker

Course Description

English 1311: Expository English Composition is the first semester course in a two-semester first-year composition (FYC) sequence. Both ENG 1311 and its second-semester counterpart, ENG 1312, are required for all students unless they have transfer credit covering this requirement or place out of one or both of the courses via the College-Level Examination Program (CLEP) exam. ENG 1311 is described in the course catalogue as a course that provides "Instruction in addressing academic writing tasks through the composing process, with emphasis on strategic use of language, of rhetorical form, and of authorial voice and point of view to inform and persuade effectively; development of critical thought through writing and reading complex discourse" (436). When I taught the course discussed here, most 1311 courses were still being taught in a very traditional FYC manner, based around a textbook with readings, and four essays based on the EDNA model: expository, descriptive, narrative, and analytical.

The course I describe here was an experimental redesign of the traditional course that was taught to two sections in Spring 2009. It took a very different approach, eschewing a textbook in favor of readings from Rhetoric and Writing Studies (RWS)[1] journals along with Internet media such as editorials and news articles. Instead of the four traditional FYC essays mentioned above, students' major assignments consisted of a summary of a Rhetoric and Writing Studies article, a contrastive rhetorical analysis, a collaborative wiki project illustrating students' understanding of the theory of epistemic rhetoric, and an end of semester reflective paper that required students to discuss how the discourses they were exposed to during the course changed their understanding of writing.

Institutional Context

The University of Texas at El Paso (UTEP) is a 20,000 student minority-majority institution located on the U.S.-Mexico border. Over 70% of the university is Latino, and Spanish is commonly heard in public spaces on campus (Center for Institutional Evaluation). An additional 9% of the students are classified as international students from Mexico, many of them crossing the border from Juárez every day to attend classes. UTEP draws the vast majority of its students from the El Paso/Juárez region, with a small percentage from other states and other countries. Due to this unique location, multilingualism is the norm and the majority of students in FYC classes have oral fluency but not necessarily full literacy in multiple languages. A minority of students are English monolinguals, others speak English as a second language, while others have grown up speaking both English and Spanish.

There has been a lot of change in UTEP's FYC courses over the past several years due to the innovative work of the current FYC Director. One of the Director's prerogatives has been to design the courses more in line with RWS as opposed to that of English literature studies, which has traditionally been a dominant influence in the design of FYC courses. When the course described here was taught, the second semester ENG 1312 had been redesigned and was just moving beyond the piloting stage. ENG 1311 was up for redesign but still based on a model that had prevailed for decades at UTEP, which loosely focused on teaching the four modes via traditional paper-based essays: expository, descriptive, narrative, and analytical. In contrast, ENG 1312 was focused on teaching for transfer, having students learn APA,[2] rather than MLA style, compose multimedia projects such as documentary videos, and use RWS disciplinary concepts (such as discourse communities) to analyze their communication networks and prepare them to enter disciplinary discourse communities. ENG 1312 was a huge step away from high school writing, which often focuses heavily on personal narrative and English literature due to a variety of reasons: state-mandated testing, mandated curriculum, and teachers' educational backgrounds in English literature and creative writing. Thus, I knew a redesigned 1311 would have to serve as a bridge between these two environments. Students' college writing would not focus on analyzing literature or writing personal narratives but would instead introduce them to disciplinary concepts and the technologies that they would need to succeed in 1312.

Some of those who teach FYC classes at UTEP are students in either the master's or doctoral programs in RWS, and they, like myself, are encouraged to incorporate RWS disciplinary knowledge in the courses they teach. However, like many universities, the majority of FYC instructors at UTEP have minimal or no background in RWS, thus limiting the amount of RWS disciplinary material that can be incorporated in any redesign. While there is a pedagogy and theory course for all new TAs that introduces them to RWS discourses, this work is not reinforced by the graduate work of most TAs in the program, who are students of literature or creative writing. As a result, the FYC Director felt that any redesign would have to adopt a specific textbook and encouraged me to try to use one within my course. My search for a textbook proved futile for a few reasons. First, there have not been any textbooks released that are suitable for a writing about writing (WAW)[3] class. Elizabeth Sargent and Cornelia Paraskevas's *Conversations about Writing—Eavesdropping, Inkshedding, and Joining In* is one possible example; however, it is a Canadian textbook that is difficult to find in the U.S. Wendy Bishop's *On Writing: A Process Reader* includes a number of essays about writing and literacy; however, they are generally popular as opposed to academic discourses about writing, which is problematic in a course designed to expose students to disciplinary discourses.[4] Textbooks often include too many readings and force an instructor down a narrow path since she feels compelled to use a book that students paid for. Choosing a textbook leaves little room to include texts related to the lives of my students, which are certainly unique given UTEP's location on the U.S.-Mexico border. For these reasons, I eschewed a traditional textbook in favor of a handbook along with articles from disciplinary journals and English and Spanish Web media sources. While this limited the possibility of such a course being adapted on a program-wide level at UTEP in the near future, I was confident that it would give a better insight regarding student ability to handle challenging disciplinary material and the value of this work, thus giving me data to argue for a more radical program-wide redesign down the line.

Theoretical Rationale

Over the past several years, interest in teaching first-year composition classes with a WAW curriculum has increased significantly. In "Language Matters: Rhetoric and Writing I as Content Course," Debra Dew explains why FYC courses at the University of Colorado-Colorado Springs moved away from the content-less FYC model to a model that used RWS disciplinary material as its content. In particular, Dew argues that the new model "restored the theoretical link between language and disciplinary content" and aligned FYC courses with other introductory courses across the disciplines, making writing instruction "more fully a scholarly enterprise with disciplinary integrity" (88). While Dew's article was published in 2003, interest in teaching FYC with a WAW focus greatly increased after the publication of Downs and Wardle's 2007 *CCC* article "Teaching About Writing, Righting Misconceptions: (Re)envisioning 'First-Year Composition' as 'Introduction to Writing Studies.'" In this article, the authors discuss what they envision as a "radically reimagined FYC" which proposes to draw on disciplinary material from writing studies to shift the focus of FYC from "teaching 'how to write in college' to teaching *about writing*—from acting as if writing is a basic, universal skill to acting as if writing studies is a discipline with content knowledge to which students should be introduced" (553).

Because Downs and Wardle's proposal is a radical departure from ways FYC has traditionally been taught, it is not surprising that their article sparked a lot of response. Libby Miles and others at the University of Rhode Island wrote a critical response to Downs and Wardle, accusing them of regressive thinking by focusing on a semester or two of FYC as opposed to pushing the development of a broader, multi-year undergraduate writing curriculum. They also suggested that FYC courses are already offering knowledge from our discipline without "miring all students in the specialized discourse of an advanced discipline" (Miles et al. 504). However, Barbara Bird has responded in support, challenging criticisms that first-year students cannot handle the difficulty of reading disciplinary discourses by explaining how she designed successful WAW classes for basic writers ("Writing").

A more recent *College Composition and Communication* article by Wardle, "'Mutt Genres' and the Goal of FYC: Can We Help Students Write the Genres of the University?," further explores the problems with traditional FYC courses and argues for the WAW approach. Here, Wardle examines a number of traditional FYC assignments, arguing that they wind up "mutt genres," "genres that do not respond to rhetorical situations requiring communication in order to accomplish a purpose that is meaningful to the author" (777). These genres, like the observation essay or the generic argument essay, do not exist in the same form outside of the FYC course. While an alternative to this would be to teach specific disciplinary genres, Wardle's discussion of an English TA attempting this approach reveals the challenges one faces in doing so. The instructor she references worked closely with a biology professor and researched the genres of the biology discourse community; however, despite this work, the TA remained a discourse community outsider and realized that she could not teach such discourses as an insider could.

I avoided "mutt genres" by having students draw on disciplinary knowledge to achieve common academic tasks. The first essay assignment asked students to compose a summary of a RWS journal article and the last asked them to reflect on their growth during the course. For the journal article summary, students performed a task that they would likely be asked to do as they progressed in their academic disciplines when they had to write an essay or a reading response. While a summary assignment may be included in a traditional FYC class, it would likely be focused on summarizing a popular text as opposed to an academic one. By having students report on an academic discourse that I am familiar with, I am in a better position to evaluate their summaries, ensuring that they captured the major points of the articles accurately in their essays.

The final essay was a reflective essay, which I used as a replacement for the traditional personal narrative essay that is included at the beginning of an FYC sequence. Whereas the typical personal narrative essay may be considered a "mutt genre" that has no real place in university-level writing,

I have found that students are often asked to reflect on their learning experiences at the end of a semester. Because this assignment required students to combine personal experience with references to academic articles, it helped prepare them for a more academic style of reflective writing than they might have engaged in previously.

My decisions in designing this course were also influenced by WAW approaches besides Downs and Wardle's. An unpublished chapter manuscript by Wardle and Downs, "Reimagining the Nature of FYC: Trends in Writing-about-Writing Pedagogies," reveals the diversity of WAW curricula that currently exists. For this chapter, they surveyed teachers utilizing WAW approaches at their universities and found three major trends:

> The first focuses on literacy and discourse, how writing and language demonstrate community membership. The second focuses on Writing Studies itself—the existence of the discipline *qua* discipline, with its knowledge and expertise on writing, emphasizing rhetorical theory and its resultant strategies for writing. The third focuses on the nature of writing and writers' practices. (15)

In Shannon Carter's Texas A&M course, students read work by scholars such as Brandt and Moss and conduct ethnographic inquiry into literacy practices in and out of school (18-19). Debra Dew's Rhetoric and Writing I: Academic Reading and Analytical Writing is a university-wide course at the University of Colorado-Colorado Springs that focuses on acknowledging Rhetoric and Writing Studies as a discipline. In this course, students read rhetorical theory and use it to analyze rhetorical performances (19-20). At Marywood University, Laurie McMillan's course uses Wendy Bishop's *On Writing: A Process Reader* and "is specifically focused on promoting transfer of knowledge gained in the class through metacognition, reflection, and explicit discussion of writing processes and practices" (20). In a recent *Basic Writing e-Journal* article ("Meaning-Making"), Barbara Bird describes her experiences teaching WAW to basic writing students at Taylor University. She focuses largely on articles that introduce students to the meaning-making power of language and includes rhetorical theorists such as Kenneth Bruffee on her reading list.

Of these approaches to WAW, my design would be most closely aligned to Dew's and Bird's models since my model takes a strong rhetorical approach, namely one that focuses on the epistemic power of rhetoric. A number of theorists like James Berlin and Kenneth Bruffee have argued for the value of a writing classroom focused on epistemic rhetoric, which postulates that "Discourse does not merely discover truth or make it effective. Discourse creates realities rather than truths about realities" (Brummett par. 20). Berlin has made the argument that rhetoric is at "the center of a culture's activities" and, as such, the teaching of rhetoric and writing is intertwined (*Writing Instruction* 2). He writes, "When freshmen [sic] learn to write or speak, they learn more than how to perform an instrumental task.... They are learning assumptions about what is real and what is illusory, how to know one from the other, how to communicate the real . . . and how language works" (2). While Writing Studies provides information about the practice of writing, such as the processes of revision, rhetorical theory provides a more complex understanding of issues such as audience consideration, exigence, *kairos*, and theories of language use. Writing Studies provides knowledge about the skills required for effective writing while Rhetoric expands on this practical knowledge by helping students understand how to make effective rhetorical choices to achieve their writing purpose.

In my course, I introduced epistemic rhetoric through the use of a video I created that focused on the way societal discourses shaped our understandings of the U.S.-Mexico border wall, a very relevant issue for the class since the border and the new wall, which some of my students crossed every day, can be seen from UTEP. The video was followed by Barry Brummett's 1977 SCA speech, "The Three Meanings of Epistemic Rhetoric." With plenty of scaffolding, my students read this speech at the beginning and end of the course. Although I knew students would struggle with the theory at first and not reach a full understanding of it in one semester, I felt that grounding the course in a theory of epistemic rhetoric gave students a better understanding of the power of rhetoric, the influence discourses had in creating their realities, and their ability to rhetorically intervene in their social and political realities. While we took different approaches in doing so, I felt I shared similar goals with Teresa Grettano who sought to "prepare [her] students to participate both as active receivers and critical senders of messages in the media circuses in which they are immersed daily" (73). Similarly, I align my goals with Barbara Bird, who says reading articles about the epistemic power of rhetoric leads students to "have a much richer, fuller understanding of the power that reader-writers exercise as they read and write" ("Meaning-Making" 3). I believed that by understanding how situatedness within certain discourses leads to a different understanding of a situation, my students would more effectively analyze the discourses surrounding them. In doing so, they might, like Grettano's and Bird's students, become more critical consumers and producers, gaining larger control over the construction of their own realities.

The influence of rhetorical theory was most evident in the second and third essay assignments in my course. The second assignment had students write an analysis of a societal issue using a theoretical framework of epistemic rhetoric while the third assignment had students compose a multimedia essay that used evidence to argue for a theory of epistemic rhetoric. With the second assignment, I worked on situating the traditional FYC rhetorical analysis more fully within RWS. Instead of limiting students to a simplistic rhetorical framework commonly found in textbooks (e.g. ethos, pathos, and logos), I had students use a more advanced theoretical framework which drew from Brummett's theory of epistemic rhetoric as well as Flower and Hass's "Reading Strategies and the Construction of Meaning." As a result, writing this analysis required students to be familiar with academic theories so that they could use them to analyze the world around them.

Heeding calls by Cynthia Selfe and Kathleeen Yancey for writing teachers to teach more than the traditional text-based essay, I made the third essay a multimedia assignment collaboratively written on a wiki. For this assignment, students built on their knowledge of epistemic rhetoric established in the first part of the semester to make an argument for this theory. Whereas a traditional FYC "mutt genre" might have students write on a generic topic such as immigration or abortion without this knowledge being situated in a particular discipline, the essay assignment in this class had students find real-world evidence to support an academic theory. This mirrors what academics do when collecting data through empirical research or discourse analysis in order to develop or support a theory.

Critical Reflection

As one who is aware of student ability to perform to the expectations of the teacher, I entered my WAW classroom with the attitude that my students, with proper scaffolding, could understand disciplinary discourses. Nonetheless, aware that I was teaching at a university with a number of students still acquiring English in addition to learning U.S. academic discourse, I wanted to design a curriculum that would be challenging but not overwhelming for my students. Thus, with the exception of the Brummett article, I began the course with older works by an accessible scholar, Donald Murray, who would help dispel student beliefs that a writing class was all about grammar while giving them knowledge about the writing process and collaboration within the writing classroom.

Compared to previous semesters of teaching FYC, teaching the course I am presenting here was a very different experience for both me and the students. This difference was evident in the student responses on the end-of-semester anonymous survey I gave, the final class evaluations, and student reflection essays.[5] In the class evaluations for the more traditional FYC course I taught the previous semester, one student stated that it felt like a high school class. In these evaluations, students mentioned nothing about the writing assignments, indicating they were a forgettable part of the course. In the evaluations of the new model, students clearly saw the course to be more rigorous, and a number of responses said the readings and the knowledge gained about RWS were the most valuable parts of the course. For instance, a student who reported liking the articles wrote, "Even though some of them were hard to understand, it really helped me overall and I know it will benefit my future education." Some survey responses for my WAW course confirmed this sentiment for traditional FYC courses and noted the difference of my new approach. One student who had previously taken 1311 wrote, "This is the second time I take ENGL 1311, and I can say that my other class was more like a high school class. We were doing very elementary things like writing about a memory, writing about our favorite things . . . ." Another student had a similar positive experience, hinting that her interest in studying writing had been strengthened through the experience: "At first I felt very discouraged to take it because it was my second time taking it and I believed that if I had no interest the first time, nothing would change the second time around. It was an extremely interesting, challenging and fun class."

As revealed by these responses and others, students found this course different from previous writing courses they had taken at both high school and college. An important difference was certainly the readings, with several students mentioning them explicitly on the end-of-semester evaluations as being one of the best parts of the course. Others mentioned how they liked the fact that RWS material was being taught in class since they had never been exposed to it before. These sentiments appeared to be reflected by a survey response in which over 35% of students said they would now be more likely to consider majoring in RWS if it was offered as a major at UTEP. The student quoted above ended his comment with, "I am not an English major, and it made me think twice about what I really wanted to major in," indicating the value of creating RWS major options. Due to our close alignment with English literature studies, this student conflated RWS with traditional English studies; however, his interest in studying English was clearly sparked by RWS disciplinary discourses.[6]

On the survey, over 80% of the students responded that the reading assignments for this course were either "More helpful" or "A lot more helpful" in improving their writing ability than those they read in previous classes, with 90% feeling the same regarding the writing assignments. Along with my students, I would argue that sustained engagement with discussions on writing helped them become better writers. This may be seen by looking at some student responses. In the end of semester reflection, Cesar wrote about his transformed understanding of the writing process:

> After reading Nancy Sommer's [sic] (1980) article, I also realized that revision by itself can be a complex process in writing. Unlike in Murray's (1972) description of revision as being part of a linear writing process, Sommer's [sic] proposes a non linear model for it. This model changed my perception of revision. I became aware that revision doesn't necessarily have to play the paper[7] of the cherry on top of the cake.

94 *Composition Studies*

As evidenced by Cesar's and other responses, students found the articles concerning revision particularly helpful. Also, as this response shows, they were able to connect ideas among various readings to analyze their own processes. Here is an example of another student, Julio, connecting readings and using them to analyze and develop his own writing processes:

> According to Murray "prewriting usually takes 85% of the writer's time" (1972, p. 90). Upon reading this I realized that I needed to begin doing some form of prewriting but I still felt that I needed to do more to my paper and I wasn't sure what it was. It wasn't until we began reading the article by Faigley & Witte did I realize that I needed to add a revision stage to my writing process and not just a editing revision process but a restructuring revision process.

It is hard to imagine that engagement with these disciplinary discourses regarding process cannot help but develop writers more effectively than the traditional content-less FYC model. As evidenced by student responses in writing and on the surveys, my students certainly saw a difference between this writing course and previous ones they had taken, understanding that the discourses on writing they read in this course helped them reflect on and develop their writing abilities in ways that anthologized popular essays could not.

The above comments reveal that students generally found readings concerned with the writing process and revision helpful and accessible; however, they were not always enthusiastic about other readings during the semester. During the class and on final evaluations, complaints about the length of the articles were fairly common even though they were never asked to read more than about ten pages of an article for a class. Overall, student reading responses revealed a fairly good understanding of the articles; however, there was consistent evidence in responses and class discussions that some students were not reading as deeply as they could. One article that students clearly did not understand well on the first reading was Brummett's, which talked about three meanings of epistemic rhetoric.[8] Virtually all of the reading responses for the initial reading were way off from understanding these distinctions; however, when we came back to it later in the semester, students' comprehension clearly improved. Julieta wrote of her transformed understanding: "The first time we read the article I was so confused by it I had no idea what he was trying to say. Now that I have a better understanding, I can imply that what he means is that, it is through the use of verbal language and communication that we create reality."

The difficulty associated with some of the more challenging readings (e.g. Brummett; Kantz; Brodkey) led at least one student to drop early in the semester. Overall, about seven out of twenty-five students (28%) from each of the two classes dropped or failed by the end of the semester, which was above the program-wide drop rate of approximately 15% (Brunk-Chavez). This higher drop rate reflects Downs and Wardle's finding that the difficulty of a WAW curriculum in which the "readings and assignments are lengthy and complex" can lead more students failing or dropping a WAW course than a traditional FYC course ("Teaching" 574). Nonetheless, my drop rate was significantly lower than that of a colleague who experimented with the WAW approach, indicating that limiting the amount of reading and choosing more accessible articles helps moderate the difficulty of the course. On the survey, more than 60% of students reported that the reading assignments were more difficult than other classes they were taking during the semester. As I struggled through discussions during some classes, it was clear that students were not always doing the readings or did not understand them well enough to discuss them confidently. When I teach a WAW class again, I will pay more attention to struggling students, pointing them to other student responses and meeting them individually or in small groups to reduce the attrition rate.

For the final course reflections, I asked students to consider "how the discourses [they] have read and discussed this semester have *recreated [their] reality* in regard to writing" (emphasis in original). While the Murray articles and the readings concerning revision were certainly popular, I was surprised at the number of students who referenced the Brummett readings as one of their favorite despite the difficulty they faced in understanding it. Cynthia titled her reflection "My metamorphosis" and explained not only the transformation she underwent in regard to writing and her view of herself as a writer, but also her view of the world around her:

> . . . our world to us is created by the knowledge we gain through discourse. With the ability to detect biases in readings or media we are no longer limited to just believing what we see or hear we have an option. I can now see the media that I had once thought was just informative is rather persuasive, and with this knowledge I do not have to fall victim to it.

Some might be apt, as Maxine Hairston or Richard Fulkerson have, to criticize a FYC course focused even partially on epistemic rhetoric, one that helps individuals become critical readers like my student Jose: "Now I understand that when I read anything it's someone else's writing and it's a tool being used to change my reality." These critics might wonder why rhetorical theory should play such a strong role in a writing classroom, worrying that teachers might become more preoccupied with indoctrinating their students than teaching writing. To challenge this, I return to the words of Cynthia, who wrote, "I as a writer can contribute to the construction of reality through participating in societal discourses. I can share and shape another person's reality." As this statement indicates, knowledge about rhetorical theory helps students understand the power of language in constructing the world around them, thus helping them realize the full potential of communicative acts like writing. With this realization, students like Cynthia and Jose may better understand the importance of being a rhetorically effective writer, something that a WAW FYC course can help them become.

While I was satisfied with how the semester went, there are multiple things that I would do differently upon teaching a WAW FYC course again. First, I would reduce the number of Murray readings since using too many of these biased students towards the expressivist paradigm early in the course. In their place, I would find other accessible articles with the help of others using the WAW approach. For instance, Barbara Bird's students have responded well to pieces such as Toby Fulwiler's "Looking and Listening for My Voice" and Mike Rose's "Rigid Rules, Inflexible Plans, and the Stifling of Language: A Cognitive Analysis of Writer's Block" (Bird, "Meaning Making"). Since most writers struggle with writer's block at some point, it is understandable that Rose's article would be interesting for students. Given the linguistically diverse student population at UTEP, I would consider including the new "CCCC Statement on Second Language Writing and Writers" and articles like Suresh Canagarajah's "Toward a Pedagogy of Shuttling Between Languages: Learning from Multilingual Writers." I would also like to focus more on the concept of "discourse communities" with David Bartholomae's often anthologized "Inventing the University." Finally, I would consider having reflective letters that draw from the course readings with each essay, instead of one reflective essay at the end. This would help students continually reflect on the knowledge gained from the readings, encouraging them to analyze and reformulate their writing processes throughout the semester.

Despite the struggles I faced while teaching this course, reading the course evaluations, survey results, and final reflections vindicated my belief that this was a more effective and more engaging way to teach writing than I had done previously. As discussed in the beginning of this section, students who found their previous English or FYC classes unhelpful or uninteresting found this curriculum engaging and helpful for their development as writers. While the director of our FYC program was clearly interested in the course I designed and enthusiastically supported my efforts, she pointed to the fact that many of the people teaching the course were not overly familiar with RWS discourses and that any upcoming 1311 redesign would need to depend on a textbook and could not expect to go as deeply into rhetorical theory and writing studies as I had done. However, as seen by the work of Elizabeth Wardle, this approach has been and can be implemented programwide, even at large universities such as the University of Central Florida, which has 45,000 students (UCF Staff). Wardle and Downs have recently published a textbook, *Writing about Writing: A College Reader*, which can help universities implement the WAW approach. While I have come to understand that rhetorical theory, an important part of the course discussed here, is not playing an important role in all WAW courses, everyone pursuing the WAW approach is making a contribution in moving beyond FYC's perpetually "intellectually thin curriculum" (Crowley 228-9) to a course that truly challenges students with intellectually demanding disciplinary content, material that better prepares students to write across a variety of academic and social contexts.

Notes

1 I am using Rhetoric and Writing Studies instead of Rhetoric and Composition because that is the name we use within our program and the one I used within my class. While many of the authors of the articles I used for my course would be more specifically situated within Composition Studies, a subset of the more encompassing Writing Studies field, I will consistently use Writing Studies to avoid any confusion that might stem from alternating between Composition Studies and Writing Studies.

2 Similarly, I required my students to use APA style. In *Composing Research*, Cindy Johanek makes a strong argument why RWS should embrace APA style over MLA style, which has traditionally dominated the RWS discipline due to its affiliation with English studies. According to Johanek, MLA treats texts as a "living object of study," which is useful for literature studies but not as useful for RWS, where texts play a different role, "constructing theory, presenting research and discussing pedagogy" (191). APA helps us focus on "not the *product* of the text that resulted from such inquiry, but on the *process* of thinking that was used to arrive at that text in the first place and the later application of those ideas to our work" (191). Similarly, as Johanek writes, the majority of students passing through FYC will be entering disciplines where they need to learn APA style. Given that they were likely exposed to MLA style through their high school English classes, FYC is a good venue to expose them to a new citation style that will likely be useful as they continue their studies.

3 While finding the label "writing about writing" problematic in that it is overly broad and also ignores rhetoric, I will use it here since it is the most commonly used term referring to FYC courses that focus on writing as a subject. As will be discussed later, WAW courses take a variety of approaches, but the approach that I focus on is one that focuses on introducing students to disciplinary discourses by treating RWS as a disciplinary community and having students read and write about the discourses in this particular community.

4 See Libby Miles's "Constructing Composition: Reproduction and WPA Agency in Textbook Publishing" for more on the limitations that Rhetoric and Composition scholars face in trying to introduce innovative ideas in textbooks.

5 This study was approved by the University of Texas at El Paso's IRB, listed under protocol #107704-2. All student names used here are pseudonyms.

6 Unfortunately, because of the lack of RWS majors within English or as a separate major, this student has the potential for disappointment if he does choose an English major, as he would be studying very different things than he did in my course. To avoid this problem, I share the hope with Downs and Wardle

that "Over time, as these groups move on to other disciplines, professions, and administrative positions, their knowledge about our field may be of assistance in creating more writing studies majors" ("Teaching" 578). This desire is not merely the selfish desire of increasing our disciplinary visibility, but stems primarily from the belief that RWS has a wealth of knowledge to teach students about writing, knowledge that they can take with them as they write in other disciplines and professions.

7 Cesar probably intended the word "role" as the Spanish equivalent is *papel*. Cesar, like many of the students in the class, was a native Spanish speaker.
8 The three meanings are: methodological, which says language is used merely to report an external truth; sociological, which argues language creates a social reality but that material reality exists outside of language; ontological, which argues that rhetoric has a role in creating all we know.

Works Cited

Bartholomae, David. "Inventing the University." *Journal of Basic Writing* 5.1 (1986): 4-23. Print.

Berlin, James A. "Poststructuralism, Cultural Studies, and the Composition Classroom: Postmodern Theory in Practice." *Rhetoric Review* 11.1 (1992): 16-33. Print.

———. "Rhetoric and Ideology in the Writing Class." *College English* 50.5 (1988): 477-94. Print.

———. *Writing Instruction in Nineteenth-Century American Colleges*. Carbondale: Southern Illinois UP, 1984. Print.

Bird, Barbara. "Meaning-Making Concepts: Basic Writer's Access to Verbal Culture." *Basic Writing e-Journal* 8 & 9 (2010): n. pag. Web. 5 June 2010.

———. "Writing about Writing as the Heart of a Writing Studies Approach to FYC: Response to Douglas Downs and Elizabeth Wardle, 'Teaching about Writing, Righting Misconceptions' and to Libby Miles et al., 'Thinking Vertically.'" *CCC* 60.1 (2008): 165-81. Print.

Bishop, Wendy. *On Writing: A Process Reader*. New York: McGraw Hill, 2003. Print.

Bruffee, Kenneth. "Social Construction, Language, and the Authority of Knowledge: A Bibliographical Essay." *College English* 48.8 (1986): 773-90. Print.

Brunk-Chavez, Beth. "Re: fyc drop rate." Message to the author. 1 Sept. 2010. E-mail.

Canagarajah, Suresh. "Toward a Writing Pedagogy of Shuttling Between Languages: Learning from Multilingual Writers. *College English* 68.6 (2006): 589-604. Print.

Center for Institutional Evaluation, Research and Planning. *The University of Texas at El Paso Fact Book 2006-2007*. The University of Texas at El Paso, 2007. Web. 1 Dec. 2008.

"CCCC Statement on Second Language Writing and Writers." *National Conference of Teachers of English*. Conference on College Composition and Communication, 2009. Web. 6 June 2010.

Crowley, Sharon. *Composition in the University: Historical and Polemical Essays*. Pittsburgh: U of Pittsburgh P, 1998. Print.

Dew, Debra. "Language Matters: Rhetoric and Writing I as Content Course." *Writing Program Administration* 26.3 (2003): 87-104. Print.

Downs, Douglas, and Elizabeth Wardle. "Teaching about Writing, Righting Misconceptions: (Re)envisioning 'First-Year Composition' as 'Introduction to Writing Studies.'" *CCC* 58.4 (2007): 552-84. Print.

Fulkerson, Richard. "Composition at the Turn of the Twenty-First Century." *CCC* 56.4 (2005): 654-87. Print.

Fulwiler, Toby. "Looking and Listening for My Voice." *CCC* 41.2 (1990): 214-20. Print.

Grettano, Teresa. "English 283: Rhetorical Theory and Applications: 'Rhetorical Theory, Mass Media, and Public Discourse.'" *Composition Studies* 36.1 (2008): 69-82. Print.

Hairston, Maxine. "Diversity, Ideology, and Teaching Writing." *CCC* 43.2 (1992): 179-93. Print.

Johanek, Cindy. *Composing Research: A Contextualist Paradigm for Rhetoric and Composition*. Logan: Utah State UP, 2000. Print.

Miles, Libby, et al. "Interchanges: Commenting on Douglas Downs and Elizabeth Wardle's 'Teaching about Writing, Righting Misconceptions.'" *CCC* 59.3 (2008): 503-12. Print.

Miles, Libby. "Constructing Composition: Reproduction and WPA Agency in Textbook Publishing." *Writing Program Administration* 24.1-2 (2000): 27-51. Print.

Rose, Mike. "Rigid Rules, Inflexible Plans, and the Stifling of Language: A Cognitivist Analysis of Writer's Block." *CCC* 31.4 (1980): 389-401. Print.

Sargent, M. Elizabeth, and Cornelia C. Paraskevas. *Conversations about Writing—Eavesdropping, Inkshedding, and Joining In*. Scarborough: Nelson Education, 2005. Print.

Selfe, Cynthia. "Technology and Literacy: A Story About the Perils of Not Paying Attention." *CCC* 50.3 (1999): 411-36. Print.

UCF Staff. "Smaller Classes, Innovative Pedagogy at UCF." *UCF Today*. 22 June 2010. Web. 9 Jan. 2011.

University of Texas at El Paso. *2006-2008 Undergraduate Catalog*. El Paso: U of Texas at El Paso, 2006. Print.

Wardle, Elizabeth. "'Mutt Genres' and the Goal of FYC: Can We Help Students Write the Genres of the University?" *CCC* 60.4 (2009): 765-89. Print.

Wardle, Elizabeth, and Doug Downs. "Reimagining the Nature of FYC: Trends in Writing-about-Writing Pedagogies." *Exploring Composition Studies: Sites, Issues, and Perspectives*. Ed. Kelly Ritter. Logan: Utah State UP, in press.

———. *Writing about Writing: A College Reader*. Boston: Bedford/St. Martin's, 2011. Print.

Yancey, Kathleen. "Made Not Only in Words: Composition in a New Key." *CCC* 56.2 (2004): 297-328. Print.

Syllabus

ENG 1311: Expository English Composition or Intro to Rhetoric and Writing Studies (RWS)

Course description and goals:
A writing class should be about writing. Unfortunately, most textbook publishers do not share this belief and choose to design books with short and superficial discussions about writing accompanied by a number of popular nonfiction essays on a wide variety of societal topics. This course will offer something different by focusing on material from rhetoric and writing studies (RWS) journals, with the belief that your engagement with discussions on writing will help you become a better writer. With that in mind, this course intends to help you do the following:
- see how writing is a process and develop this process
- explore the concept of "discourse community" and gain a basic understanding of the RWS discourse community
- learn to read more critically and effectively question texts and the ideologies behind them
- learn how to read and effectively give feedback on another's writing through peer review
- examine and improve your own revision process
- understand what "rhetoric" is and why it is important for you
- develop technological literacy through the use of multiple online technologies
- reflect on your growth as a writer

Required texts:
- Faigley, L. (2007). *The brief Penguin handbook*. New York, Pearson/Longman.

Printed copies of the following articles, which may be found on Blackboard and in the library databases:

- Brodkey, L. (1989). Transvaluing difference. *College English, 51.6*, 597-601.
- Brummett, B. (1979). Three meanings of epistemic rhetoric. *Speech Communication Association Annual Conference*, San Antonio, Texas.
- Emig, J. (1977). Writing as a mode of learning. *College Composition and Communication, 28.2*, 122-128.
- Faigley, L. & Witte, S. (1981). Analyzing revision. *College Composition and Communication, 32.4*, 400-414.

- Hass, C. & Flower, L. (1988). Rhetorical reading strategies and the construction of meaning. *College Composition and Communication, 39.2*, 167-83.
- Kantz, M. (1990). Helping students use textual sources persuasively. *College English, 52.1*, 74-91.
- Murray, D. (1991). All writing is autobiography. *College Composition and Communication, 42.1*, 66-74.
- Murray, D. (1978). Write before writing. *College Composition and Communication, 29.4*, 375-81.
- Murray, D. (1972). Teach writing as a process not product. *The Leaflet*, 11-14.
- Murray, D. (1970). The interior view: One writer's philosophy of composition. *College Composition and Communication, 21.1*, 21-26.
- Ong, W. (1975). The writer's audience is always a fiction. *PMLA, 90.1*, 9-21.
- Sommers, N. (1980). Revision strategies of student writers and experienced adult writers. *College Composition and Communication, 31.4*, 378-88.

Assignments:

1) Readings: These include the articles listed at the beginning of this syllabus as well as from the required *Brief Penguin Handbook* and various web articles assigned throughout the course.

2) Online postings, Journals, and Peer Review: You will complete online responses to the readings at least once a week, with details about these assignments given in the daily calendar. Additionally, you will be asked to read and respond to your peers' work in various peer review assignments throughout the course.

3) In-class Writing: On days where there is no response assignment, you may be asked to write about the reading in class. We will also use class time for researching and drafting essay assignments.

4) Essay 1 (Summary): Throughout college, you may often be asked to summarize sources in informal class responses or in writing more formal essays. While it is impossible to be completely unbiased, Faigley's (2009) Handbook describes how the writer of a summary should give the appearance of neutrality in its description of the difference between a summary and an analysis. For this essay, you need to choose one of four RWS articles that I have posted on Blackboard:
>Janet Emig's "Writing as a Mode of Learning"
>Donald M. Murray's "All Writing Is Autobiography"
>Walter J. Ong's "The Writer's Audience Is Always a Fiction"
>Gordon Rohman's "Pre-writing the Stage of Discovery in the Writing Process"

and write a summary for a student in another composition class that did not have the chance to read the article you did. You should use the questions I provide to help guide you in planning your summary.

5) Essay 2 (Rhetorical Analysis): In the last essay, you wrote a summary of one of the articles we read earlier in the semester. In that summary, your goal was, as described by Flower and Hass (1988), mainly "creating a gist and paraphrasing content"; however, while your writing in this essay may include some summary, your task in this assignment goes beyond that. The difference between the two tasks may be connected to the difference between the work of student and experienced writers in the Hass and Flower study: "While the student reader is mainly creating a gist and paraphrasing content, the experienced reader does this and more—he then tries to infer the author's purpose and even creates a sort of strident persona for the writer" (p. 177). Once you select your texts, you will write a comparative rhetorical analysis, comparing and contrasting the authors' and/or newspaper's ideological leanings and how they affect the delivery of their message.

6) Essay 3 (Wiki): For this essay, you are going to illustrate the notion that rhetoric is epistemic, that discourse creates our realities. In order to do this, you have three options: (1) select multiple texts on a single public issue such as the U.S.-Mexico border wall. Using text, video, pictures, and audio, you will illustrate how the issue is represented differently by different people and how their views are a reflection of ideological bias; (2) show how the Internet allows us to construct our own realities by giving us more power to choose the discourses we consume and contribute to public discourses through sharing on sites like Facebook; and (3) create an iMovie like the one we watched on the U.S.-Mexico border wall. The movie can focus on one of the two assignments listed above.

7) Essay #3 Oral Presentation: For our final exam period, you will work with your partner to prepare a short presentation (approx. 5-10 minutes) in which you discuss your wiki essay. You should plan to show us your essay, provide some details about your writing process, discuss what your essay is about, and explain why the visual elements are important to it.

8) End of Semester Reflection: Most likely, this class was different from other writing-oriented classes that you have taken. Over the course of the semester, we will read a number of articles from Rhetoric and Writing Studies journals discussing issues such as writers' processes, revising effectively, reading rhetorically, and even the construction of knowledge. As cited in the prompt for Essay #3, Brummett (1977) said, "Discourse does not merely discover truth or make it effective. Discourse creates realities rather than truths about realities." For this reflective

essay, I would like you to consider the above quote and think about how the discourses you have read and discussed this semester have *recreated your reality* in regard to writing. The most successful reflections will demonstrate thoughtful consideration of the work we have done this semester. Reflections of this nature will (1) contain specific references to and quotes from multiple texts that we have read, (2) mention specific writing tasks that were particularly helpful in your growth as a writer, and (3) speculate on how this growth will be helpful in your future writing endeavors both inside and outside the classroom.

Grading:

You will have three major types of graded assignments for this course: essays, daily homework assignments, and reading quizzes. The essays will be evaluated on a traditional 100 pt. scale. All other assignments (homework responses, in-class quizzes, peer review responses, online skill-building, and others) will be evaluated on a 5 pt. scale. For reading responses, a typical 5 pt. response will include a well-thought out response that responds to the question asked and proper APA citation with at least one quote from the reading.

>Final grades will be calculated as follows:
>Essay #1: 15%
>Essay #2: 15%
>Essay #3: 15%
>End of semester reflection: 15%
>Online postings, homework assignments, quizzes, and peer review: 25%
>Classroom community building (class participation, motivation, and general enthusiasm): 10%
>Oral presentation during exam period: 5%

Bullet key for calendar
- ✎ Class Activity/Note
- ✍ Writing Assignment
- 📖 Reading Assignment

Day 1
- ✎ Introductions and class policies
- ✎ In-class writing and group discussions on expectations

Day 2
- 📖 Read syllabus
- ✍ Type, print, and bring to class a 150-word response to this question: Upon reading the syllabus, how does this writing class look different from previous ones you've taken?

- ✎ Introduction to rhetoric as epistemic
    Day 3
- 📖 Download from Blackboard, print, and read Barry Brummett's "Three Meanings of Epistemic Rhetoric."
- ✍ On WebCT, post a 150-word response describing the difference **in your own words** between the three notions of rhetoric as epistemic that Brummett describes.
- ✎ Introduction of the rhetorical triangle.
    Day 4
- 📖 Download from WebCT, print, and read Donald Murray's 1970 article "The interior view: One writer's philosophy of composition."
- ✍ On Blackboard, post a 150-word response explaining how this reading helped expand your understanding of the rhetorical triangle introduced on Monday and described on p. 1 of the Handbook.
    Day 5
- 📖 Download from Blackboard, print, and read Murray's "Teaching writing as a process not product."
- ✍ On Blackboard, post a 150-word response to **one** of these two questions: (1) How does Murray's advice for teaching differ from previous writing instruction you've had? OR (2) Murray explains that each part of the process takes different amounts of time. According to Murray, what part takes the most time? Why do you think this is?
    Day 6
- ✍ Type, print, and bring to class a single-spaced 400-600 word reflection on how your process compares to that described by Murray (note: this counts as two homework assignment grades). Use the following questions to guide your reflection:
    - What process do you use when writing? How does this change if you're writing an academic essay as opposed to an email?
    - What is the most time consuming part of your process? The least?
    - What is the most difficult part of your process?
    - Which of Murray's implications did you find most important?
    Day 7
- 📖 Read Handbook pp. 297-299 and pp. 321-330. On pp. 321-330, pay more attention to the use of APA style as opposed to the content of the paper. How does the writer integrate quotes and cite them? How is the paper formatted? How are the references listed?

- Revise one of your Murray postings by adding at least one properly integrated and cited quote and including a reference list that lists Murray's article properly. Print and bring to class. **Note: from this point on, you should always use proper APA style in your online postings and any source-based writing you do for this class.**

Day 8
- Complete "APA Citations" exercise online using the Handbook to help you.
- Read Handbook pp. 6-19, "Planning and drafting," and consider the following question when reading: How did this reading help you better understand Murray's assertion that pre-writing should be the most time consuming part of the writing process?

Day 9
- Download from Blackboard, print, and read Donald Murray's 1978 article "Write before writing."
- On Blackboard, post a 150-word response to **one** of the following: (1) Using a personal experience with a previous writing task, help clarify the connection between increasing information and increasing concern OR (2) Think of an important piece of writing you've done. Describe how two of Murray's signals (like genre) were particularly important for your writing.

Day 10
- Read the assignment prompt for Essay #1, Handbook pp. 75-79, and the sample essay posted on Blackboard (a summary of Gordon Rohman's 1965 article "Pre-writing the stage of discovery in the writing process").
- Write a 200-300 word response answering the questions that are posted on Blackboard about the sample summary essay you read.
- Introduce Essay #1

Day 11
- Read through your previous responses and glance at the articles we've read to decide which one interested you the most.
- Reread the article you chose and take notes based on the Essay #1 assignment prompt. Bring both the article and notes to class.
- In-class pre-writing exercises.
- Sign up for group conferences – you need to post a draft of your essay on Blackboard under your group number under "Peer Review Conferences" **24 hours before your conference** so your peers and I have time to read your essay.

Day 12
- Read Handbook pp. 218-224, "Avoiding plagiarism."
- Complete "Planning Essay #1" exercise online.

- ✒ In-class activities on summarizing and paraphrasing.
  Day 13
- 📖 **Small group conferences on drafts in the Writing Center** – follow the directions on Blackboard to post your essay at least 24 hours before the conference, read your partners' essays, and post your comments before the session.
  Day 14
- 📖 **Essay #1 due—submit online by class time**
- 📚 Read Handbook pp. 47-55, "Read and view with a critical eye" and consider the following questions while reading: When reading, do you follow the suggestions given? If not, what did you learn while reading that could help you read more actively?
  Day 15
- 📚 Download from Blackboard, print, and read Christina Haas and Linda Flower's 1988 article "Reading strategies and the construction of meaning" to p. 174. Consider the following questions when reading: (1) How is viewing meaning as "a rich network of disparate kinds of information" (p. 170) different from other types of reading for meaning that students may be asked to do? AND (2) According to Hass and Flower, why might different readers understand a text in different ways?
  Day 16
- 📚 Read the rest of Hass and Flower's article and consider the following questions when reading: (1) What does it mean to view texts as discourse acts? and (2) How do writers who write rhetorically differ from those who don't?
  Day 17
- ✒ Return Essay #1, summarize feedback, and have a revision workshop in which the class works together on revising one essay.
  Day 18
- 📚 Read Handbook pp. 404-413 and read your essay, looking for these errors.
- 📖 Complete the "Editing" assignment online using Essay #1.
- ✒ In-class work on comma errors.
  Day 19
- 📖 Complete the comma exercise assigned online.
- 📖 On Blackboard, post a 150-word response to the following question: How can reading rhetorically make you a better writer? Use at least one quote from the Hass and Flower article in your response.
  Day 20
- 📚 Read the assignment prompt for Essay #2, a comparative rhetorical analysis, and the Handbook pp. 55-66, "Write to Analyze."

- ✎ Evaluate the Handbook's sample essay (on pp. 60-66) by posting a response to the questions on Blackboard.
- ✗ Introduce Essay #2

   Day 21 – **at a conference – no F2F class**
- 📖 Read an editorial in a newspaper at a site like nytimes.com, guardian.co.uk, or elpasotimes.com.
- ✎ Post a 200-word response in which you analyze the author of the editorial. Use the following questions to guide you: (1) What purpose does the writer have for writing?, (2) What assumptions does the writer make?, and (3) Where would you situate the writer on the political spectrum? Liberal, centrist, conservative or somewhere in between?

   Day 22– **at a conference – no F2F class**
- 📖 Choose and read one of the pairs of news articles I will post on Blackboard.
- ✎ Post a 300-word response in which you analyze how the articles present different views on the news issue being discussed. Use the following questions to guide you: (1) How do the articles report the issue differently?, (2) How might this difference be affected by the location of the author of the article or the newspaper in which it's published?, and (3) Many assume that news articles are "objective" representations of reality. How does your reading of the pair of articles you selected challenge this view?

   Day 23
- 📖 Find, print, and read two articles, editorials, or speeches on the same topic (expect to use these for Essay #2). Bring them to class.
- ✎ On Blackboard, post a 300-word response in which you analyze the articles using the questions in the Day 21 assignment.

   Day 24
- ✎ Complete the "Essay #2 Outline" exercise online by posting an outline that details the main points of your essay. Look at the samples in the Handbook on pp. 17-18 and the assignment online and decide how you want to format your outline.

   Day 25
- ✎ By 5 p.m. Friday, post a draft of your essay under Essay #2 Peer Review and your group number on Blackboard. Follow the instructions online to post your essay and your comments before Monday's class.

   Day 26
- ✎ Follow the instructions online to complete peer reviews by this class period. In class, you will meet F2F to discuss online comments.

   Day 27

- Download from Blackboard, print, and read Nancy Sommers's 1980 article "Revision strategies of student writers and experienced adult writers."
- Post a 200-word response on Blackboard responding to the following questions: What are the differences that Sommers finds between the revisions made by student and experienced writers? Where would you place yourself in relation to the writers Sommers describes?
  Day 28
- **Submit Essay #2 on Blackboard by class time.**
- Download from Blackboard, print, and read Lester Faigley and Stephen Witte's 1981 article "Analyzing revision" to p. 405. Consider the following two questions while reading: (1) What is the difference between meaning changes and surface changes? and (2) What is the difference between macrostructure and microstructure changes?
  Day 29
- Finish reading the Faigley and Witte article and consider the following two questions while reading: (1) Which group made the highest percentage of meaning changes? The least? Why do you think this is? and (2) According to the authors, why did the more advanced writers possibly make fewer overall revisions?
  Day 30
- In-class revision workshop on Essay #2.
  Day 31
- Join PBWiki and view the video on the class wiki's homepage. As you view the video, consider the argument that the video makes and whether or not you agree with it.
  Day 32
- Reread Brummett's "Three meanings of epistemic rhetoric," found on Blackboard.
- On Blackboard, post a 200-word response explaining how your understanding of Brummett's article has changed since you read it earlier in the semester.
  Day 33
- Read "Rhetoric as epistemic: What's the big deal?" on the class wiki. Consider the following questions when reading: (1) Why do the authors of this text object to Hairston's argument that instructors should not let ideology influence writing classroom design? and (2) How has technology enabled students to create knowledge through participation in societal discourse?
- **Revision of Essay #2 due by class time**
  Day 34

- Download from Blackboard, print, and read Margaret Kantz's 1990 article "Using textual sources persuasively" to p. 79. Consider the following question while reading: How was Shirley's original treatment of the topic different from what her friend suggested?
  Day 35
- Finish the Kantz article
- On Blackboard, post a 150-word response to the following question: How is the paragraph that starts at the bottom of p. 81 that begins "Alice, who thinks rhetorically…" indicate that Kantz believes in the notion of rhetoric as epistemic?
  Day 36
- Log onto the wiki and read the assignment prompt for Essay #3.
- Complete the Freewriting assignment online as a way to brainstorm for Essay #3. Submit online, print your freewrite, and bring it to class.
- Introduce Essay #3.
- In-class: (1) Pick a partner, (2) share your freewriting/brainstorm topics and discuss ways you could develop them, and (3) decide on a topic.
  Day 37
- Read back over the Brummett article and the wiki pages we read and pick quotes that can be helpful for your essay. Post these on your wiki page.
- In computer classroom with partner: Find at least two discourse sources on your topic, discuss how they offer different perspectives on your issue, and post a 150-word summary of your discussion on your wiki page.
  Day 38
- Download from Blackboard, print, and read Linda Brodkey's 1989 article "Transvaluing Difference." Consider the following questions when reading: (1) Where would you situate Brodkey on the political spectrum? What ideologies does she espouse? (2) On p. 598, what false assumption does Brodkey say students and colleagues often make? and (3) Based on her discussion on the bottom of p. 599, what does Brodkey think about objectivity?
- On your essay page, post at least one quote from this article that can be helpful for your paper, explaining how you might use it.
  Day 39
- Post at least two more discourse sources/examples that you can use for your essay.
- In-class partner work: Develop an outline for your essay using the quotes and discourse sources you have collected on your wiki page.

Day 40
- In-class descriptions of work in progress—briefly explain the outlines you developed, focusing on the point of your essay and what specific examples you are going to do to develop that point.

Day 41
- Have essay drafted by this class period. Will meet in computer classroom for peer review.

Day 42
- Introduce end of semester reflection assignment: As cited in the prompt for Essay #3, Brummett (1977) said, "Discourse does not merely discover truth or make it effective. Discourse creates realities rather than truths about realities." For this reflective essay, I would like you to consider the above quote and think about how the discourses you have read and discussed this semester have *recreated your reality* in regard to writing.
- Class evaluations.

Submit Essay #3 and the end of semester reflection on Blackboard by the exam period.

Graduate Study at Arizona State University
DEPARTMENT OF ENGLISH
MA Rhetoric and Composition
PhD Rhetoric, Composition, and Linguistics

FACULTY

Patricia Boyd | Alice Daer | James Gee | Maureen Daly Goggin (Chair)
Peter Goggin | Elisabeth Hayes | Kathleen Lamp | Elenore Long
Paul Kei Matsuda | Keith Miller | Ersula Ore | Shirley Rose | Doris Warriner

The Department of English at ASU has created a diverse and energetic intellectual atmosphere within which to pursue graduate studies. Boasting one of the largest, most productive faculties in the western United States, the department is highly regarded for its professional development and mentoring programs, which prepare students for successful careers in academia and beyond.

english.clas.asu.edu/graduate

DEPARTMENT OF WRITING STUDIES
UNIVERSITY OF MINNESOTA

Study at a research-intensive university with an internationally recognized faculty in one of the longest established rhetoric & scientific and technical communication programs in the country. In addition to our rich history, we have a new commitment to Writing Studies as a field involving research and teaching about global, social, and the digital dimensions of writing.

M.A. and Ph.D. Degrees in Rhetoric and Scientific and Technical Communication
Our program combines theory and research in all aspects of writing, rhetoric, and technical communication. The Ph.D. is in high demand; all of our graduates have placed in academic or industry positions.

M.S. and B.S. Degrees in Scientific and Technical Communication and the Technical Communication Certificate
Designed for working professionals and other students whose primary goal is a career in the field of technical communication.

To find out more visit www.writingstudies.umn.edu

Mestiz@ Scripts, Digital Migrations, and the Territories of Writing, by Damián Baca. New York: Palgrave McMillan, 2008. 240 pp.

Reviewed by Valerie Balester, Texas A&M University

If you think you know the history of rhetoric, think again. You may be deluded. In fact, if you think you can teach the history of rhetoric, you may, like I did after reading this book, decide you need to start all over again, that what you in fact know is a very tiny sliver of the world's traditions. Much of the last thirty years of scholarship has recovered women rhetoricians within the framework of Western and European traditions from classical Greece to modern America, but has yet to consider seriously rhetorics of other traditions. Damián Baca begins to chart these new territories for us with *Mestiz@ Scripts, Digital Migrations, and the Territories of Writing*. Reading the book is much like taking a journey, both spatially and temporally. You may have a vague sense that Mesoamerican civilization before the conquistadors was sophisticated and that it was trampled upon by Cortez and his ilk. However, unless you have read widely in the history of the pre-1630 Mesoamerican civilizations, you may also believe they were preliterate, or that they were destroyed and erased by conquest. In fact, theirs is a story of adaptation and survival through syncretism—a slow process of melding cultures. Baca argues that Mesoamerican civilizations can point the way to a twenty-first-century re-reading of literacy, rhetorical history, and composition practice. Using Gloria Anzaldúa's concepts of borderlands, contact zones, and new *mestiz@* consciousness, he re-configures the territory of rhetoric.

In his first chapter, Baca outlines his main arguments and previews the upcoming chapters. The cross-cultural contact between the Spanish from the Iberian Peninsula and the American Indians (including North America, Mesoamerica, and the Caribbean) in the late-fifteenth century resulted in a hybrid, or *mestiz*, culture. Mestiz culture has been marked by adaptive resistance to erasure and assimilation, as expressed in part by expressive culture, including performance, art, and writing, often in combination. The rhetoric of mestiz@ culture is not simply persuasive. It is epistemic, a way to convey, preserve, and express cultural norms and identity; it mediates between cultures. When we shift our definitions of literacy to include practices outside the alphabetic version and beyond academic prose, to include, for example, the performances that accompanied texts or to include pictographic or mural representations, we approach a consciousness that will help us navigate and understand literacy in the twenty-first century. So, for example, Baca explains in chapter 4 the power of the pictographic script, its ability to convey multiple and complex culturally embedded meanings, or the ritualistic and ceremonial means by which official discourse was presented and conveyed (poetry, prayer, oration, script). In the opening chapter, Baca also explains the word *mestiz@*. The addition of @ makes the term gender inclusive, although it may take you a few chapters to become accustomed to the new convention. I advise you to get used to a bit of discomfort. It will be worth it. This read will take you to decidedly new places.

One of those places is the Mesoamerican civilization of the Olmec, in the tropical lowlands of Mexico from about 1300 BCE, some 3,300 years ago. Chapters 2 and 3 critically review much of the literature on mestiz@ history, myth, and culture, providing a rich historical perspective on Mesoamerican/Indian literacy education and practices, all the while making the argument for a "new consciousness" based on more than simple alphabetic literacy. Baca describes how, for example, the Olmec literacy was grounded in calendars and glyphic inscriptions, the meaning of which remains somewhat mysterious. A little known literacy practice of the Inca civilization that flourished between 1200 CE through the conquest of the 1530s were the color-coded knotted cords, or *khipu*, used to convey information. The Mayan civilization of the Yucatán perfected hieroglyphic scripts (as well as calendars, astronomy, and architecture). The word "Mexican" is from the Aztec, or *Culhua-Mexica* ("Me-shee-kah") civilization, whose great city of Tenochtitlán boasted 300,000 inhabitants and a complex architecture and civic/political/economic structure by the time of conquest. They used pictographic forms of literacy that recorded their origin myths, royal lineages, and business. This civilization, ruled by Moctezuma, survives most strongly in mestiz@ identity through cultural practices never entirely erased despite centuries of oppression. Chapter 3, "A Brief History, From Mexicatl to Chican@," traces their influence all the way to the Chican@ movement of the twentieth century.

Besides a geographical re-examination, Baca invites us to reconsider alphabetic and academic literacy by looking back to the history of Mesoamerican writing practices that encompassed picture, symbol, and performance. He makes a connection to multimedia and new literacy, both in the sense of genre and in the way it can and should contest the binaries of dominant historical narratives through its play with doubling, twinning, and pairing. He does this in part by analyzing, especially in chapters 4 and 5, modern-day mestiz@ texts such as the 2000 *Codex Espangliensis: from Columbus to the Border Partol*, the work of three artists, an illustrator, a graphic designer, and a performance artist. (I recommend you check it out online at movingpartspress.com.) Chapter 5 brings visual rhetoric into the argument, with special attention to how cultures gradually adapted and merged and transgressed borders through works such as Frederico Virgil's mural at the Barelas-Albuquerque's National Hispanic Cultural Center, *The Genesis of the Rio Grande*. The reading Baca gives of the mural clarifies how Mesoamerican culture has survived, adapted, and resisted assimilation, in living color.

In chapters 6 and 7, Baca makes two challenges, one to the history of rhetoric as it is commonly found in the curriculum of higher education, and another that I personally found even more intriguing, the challenge to our writing pedagogy. In the classroom, he pushes us to read culture—including music, dance, painting, and writing—with an eye to how cultures are enacted in these works. He calls for a more deeply critical reading of texts (and I include here many kinds of texts) within a cultural context—not simply a Western cultural context. Mestiz@ texts are particularly instructive in that they provide a study of survival, having continually adapted and crossed between Western and Mesoamerican rhetorical practices. Some of the texts that best illustrate this adaptive strategy are not what we have, in rhetorical studies, always acknowledged as text—pictographs, hieroglyphs, codex writing, frescos, and ceremonial dance—and these are forms still being produced by mestiz@ rhetoricians.

In many college classrooms, these texts are invisible, as are the writers and artists who produce them. While composition classes can be constructed to accomplish assimilation, thus erasing these texts, reading (or seeing or hearing) them makes us confront their makers' resistance, subversion, and adaptation—often geared at survival.

Baca implies, but does not cover in depth, the need to re-imagine the production of texts by students in classrooms. Naturally, we want to approach students of mestiz@ backgrounds with a respect for the rhetorical traditions of their ancestors. We want to help them reclaim those rhetorics, to correct some of the violence of school histories that ignore them or treat them as preliterate barbarians who were bettered by having been conquered by a more "advanced" civilization. We just as urgently need to educate European/Anglo students about this history and about the other versions of rhetoric that exist in the Americas (the Asian, non-mestiz@ Native American, and African American as well). By importing Anzaldúa's new mestiz@ consciousness, Baca suggests we can reach students as rhetoricians and writers in a whole new way. Writing is not simply following a set of conventions devised in seventeenth century England, not simply about the persuasive tactics devised in the Greco-Roman era. Rhetoric in the twenty-first century has to be more to survive as a subject of study. It has to take a clue from the survival tactics used by mestiz@ cultures. Moving into multimedia, entertaining different varieties of language, incorporating electronic voice or music into productions are all elements of rhetoric and "writing" that belong in our classes. Just as important is allowing texts to critique and challenge the master narratives of our culture, making space for new texts.

As Baca constructs it, it is a two-step process: revise our rhetorical history and recover what we have lost. The losses include the many students not currently being served by our education system, their ways of being, doing, knowing, and communicating. It is a wholly new understanding of American rhetoric.

At some points reading, I got the panicked feeling of ineptitude. But then I looked again at the pedagogical project Baca advocates—he stresses exploring new territories together with students, making a map, redefining and redrawing boundaries—he suggests that rhetoric is not a set of strategies and terms and dates of great masters to memorize but a dynamic practice: "Mestiza consciousness potentially reveals a new politics of teaching that no longer privileges speaking, writing, and thinking within a single language controlled by the conventions of scholarly prose" (29). It's a project we cannot afford to ignore.

College Station, TX

The Future of Invention: Rhetoric, Postmodernism, and the Problem of Change, by John Muckelbauer. Albany: SUNY P, 2008. 214 pp.

Reviewed by Trisha Red Campbell, University of Pittsburgh

The Future of Invention, though published in 2008, may serve as particularly poignant now, at a time when plagiarism appears to be at its peak, digital composing wonders how to invent, and recycled pastiche stands in for new and innovative. The question of invention sits upon compositionists' lips, yet the performance found in Muckelbauer's work does not take these issues up explicitly; rather, he artfully asks us to look at our image of invention and complicate the tendency of its negative movement—its very insistence upon negating in order to create anew. Still, Muckelbauer does not so easily lay his argument out for us, for it is precisely in his style of engagement with the reader that he performs what he is simultaneously explaining: an orientation toward affirmative invention. Muckelbauer, rather than arguing with his sources or with invention prior, engages the scholarship in an affirmative sense.

Therefore, this work proves to be particularly difficult to review (as it doesn't seem to be reviewed in any other journals) because Muckelbauer is asking us to orient ourselves differently within composing practices. He stoutly tells us that the argument, including his own, need no longer be the most important aspect to scholarship, rather it is our style of engagement, our ways of responding to problems in the first place, that may need the most attention (Introduction). Nevertheless, I will attempt to package his argument for you here, but to do so is to betray his performance and the performativity necessary in his "affirmative" sense of change.

Muckelbauer has divided his book into two parts and eight chapters therein. Part I called "Orientations" lays out the "problem of change" in chapter 1 as a theoretical, philosophical, and rhetorical question, connecting it to Schiappa's "postmodern challenge." Chapter 2, "Why Rhetoric, Which Rhetoric?" affixes the history of rhetorical invention to a series of alleged postmodern questions, further developing an affirmative sense of change. In chapter 3, "How to Extract Singular Rhythms—Affirmative Reading and Writing," Muckelbauer offers us a type of affirmative methodology, re-visiting Derrida, Nietzsche, and Deleuze for the how of their work, not the what. Here, he is less interested in what they are arguing and more interested in how they argue. The end of chapter 3 also finally gives us a hint toward the section name of "Orientations." Muckelbauer reveals that he is "avoiding orienting toward intentions"; this includes not "getting Plato right" but orienting towards what his writing does and "what it can do" (38). Part I reads as explanatory and Part II, titled "Intensities" (a Deleuzian term most easily defined as difference referring to other differences, a difference in intensity), takes that explanation and performs it demonstratively with chapter 4, "Imitation and Invention," taking up the movement directly between model and copy. Chapter 5, "Intineration—*What is a Sophist*?" performs another form of affirmative invention, where Muckelbauer follows the how of Plato's dialogue, *The Sophist*, re-orienting Plato as a "becoming-sophist" (xiv). In tracing the movement between Plato and Sophistry, he unravels the differences between the two. Chapter 6, "Situatedness and Singularity," complicates the opposition from specific to general in terms of situated audience in composition pedagogy. Instead, Muckelbauer advances a theory of kairotic composition accounting for the "singularity of actual situatedness" (115). Chapter 7, "Topoi—Replacing Aristotle," performs a reading of Aristotle's *Physics* in order to demonstrate that the confusion surrounding the notion of topoi is not confusion at all, but "gaps" that should be given attention as inventive movements. The final chapter, "The Future of Invention—Doxa and the Common," analyzes the relationship between tradition and innovation in relation to invention so that we may reconfigure futurity itself. This chapter is where the book is going all along, questioning our very relationship to the future.

In his preface, Muckelbauer echoes something we tussle with in the field of Composition and intimates where this book is situated. He writes, "so many others here and elsewhere insistently remind me of the 'practical' dimension of my 'theoretical' obsession" (vii). His work straddles this complicated edge, through the reliance upon Derrida, Nietzsche, Deleuze, and Guattari, yet it is in his title that we are struck immediately by what is practical in this work: the future of invention. Is this not a most practical question? What is the future of invention in Composition Studies?

Muckelbauer initially restates this question as the "problem of change" elsewhere referred to as the "problem of writing" by Deleuze (chapter 1). Ostensibly diverse and distinct fields of foundationalism/anti-foundationalism, humanism/postmodernism, universalism/relativism all share a common commitment to a dialectical notion of change, thereby reinfusing one of the most commonly ignored binaries, that between same and different. The problem of change then is that to make something new, different, or even original, it must negate something else. The innovative (the different) negates the traditional (the same), which is precisely how it becomes the innovative. A classical example is that between Plato and the Sophists, often taken up in rhetorical scholarship. By reversing which position is privileged, we certainly do get a new take, yet we do so only by reproducing the same system, the same dialectic of negation. This exchange is well known; the group occupying the positions may change, but the positions are the same. This is the problem of change. Muckelbauer performatively asks us to look away from these points of opposition, and to instead look at the particular movement of negation between the points (chapter 4 and 5). It is movement that Muckelbauer is most compelled by, for it is movement that keeps binaries within negation and it is yet again movement in another direction, which creates the affirmative (chapter 2). Muckelbauer chooses rhetoric because it is the art of persuasion and the process of investigating the "asignifying" aspects of language (chapter 2). Thus rhetorical invention is somewhere between signification and non-signification and is integral to this other kind of change (not to be confused with a new kind of change, because that would be a negation). Muckelbauer calls this change affirmative, which is a post-dialectical/post-negation style of change. The opportunity of responding differently in any particular occurrence is crucial—he wants to design and invent the potential of responding without negation (chapter 3).

The Future of Invention may not be a typical argument and a certain amount of patience is required to extract Muckelbauer's own singular rhythms (chapter 3). He uses Deleuzian terms coupled with his own lucid explanation, followed by a display of the explanation. His writing mimics a philosophical style, and at times, I desperately wished for the display to cease. However, because he is asking us to engage differently with texts and with composing, I found it easier to read on, attempting to perform an affirmative reading strategy. Each chapter builds upon this other kind of invention and by the end we're left with the most compelling moment of the whole book. What is the future of rhetorical invention? "To speak of the future of invention, then, is not to refer to what comes next for invention . . . because tradition is nothing other than its own self-overcoming" (165). Instead, the future of invention within the tension between tradition and innovation offers something much more supple (chapter 8). Within the movement between tradition and innovation the future is both unrecognizable and only actualized through recognition (165). Muckelbauer asks us to follow the "singular rhythm" of futurity, the outgrowth of this movement to the very possibility of beginning.

The practical reader may not be fully convinced, however. I am not yet sure myself how to thoroughly enact Muckelbauer's philosophy, although I do see a call for rhetorical invention that speaks to our current moment as necessary. Because Muckelbauer rarely breaks from his philosophical prose, our only sense of clear application comes in chapter 6, where he raises serious questions about the teaching of situated audiences. And, in an entire book written about invention, he never once mentions digital composing. I suppose that leaves us wondering how *The Future of Invention* changes composing practices. What I see as most relevant is Muckelbauer's sense of "singular rhythms"; these are the lines and movements that don't fit into points, but rather outgrow the points. Singular rhythms are the differences in each repetition, movement, and argument. They are relevant for what they offer methodologically, which suggests we could draw attention to the movement between points, between binaries, in order to attain an affirmative invention. Yet, it is to digitality and digital composing that I think Muckelbauer's work most pertains to, as a site of constant movement, allowing composing to evolve out of the movement.

Taken as a whole, *The Future of Invention* fluently mingles invention, binaries, composition, writing, and change in a way that allows the reader to follow Muckelbauer's *movement* across concepts and to envision a practical dimension to his theoretical obsession. It begs for further readings along with pedagogical and scholarly application.

Pittsburgh, PA

Genre in a Changing World, edited by Charles Bazerman, Adair Bonini, and Débora Figueiredo. Fort Collins: WAC Clearinghouse; West Lafayette: Parlor, 2010. 528 pp.

Reviewed by Kerry Dirk, Virginia Tech

In 1997, Charles Bazerman claimed that "Genres are forms of life, ways of being. . . . Genres are the familiar places we go to create intelligible communicative action with each other and the guideposts we use to explore the familiar" (19). Years later, perhaps to illustrate just how genres can make communication understandable, Bazerman, along with Adair Bonini and Debora Figueiredo, have compiled a collection of 24 chapters in *Genre in a Changing World*. Chosen from the conference presentations at the Fourth International Symposium on Genre Studies (SIGET IV) in Brazil, the chapters represent work from a multitude of countries, including the United States, Brazil, Australia, Canada, Chile, Finland, France, Portugal, the UK, and Argentina. The second book to come from a SIGET conference, the editors argue in their introduction that "all regions of the world are increasingly aware that they are caught up in a global information economy" and thus "people of all nations need to be able to communicate in specialized professional realms" (ix-x). What one can especially appreciate about this book is the plurality of voices that are represented in this international perspective, allowing especially those well versed in genre theory to see what work is being done outside of the United States. Further, this book brings together the ESP Tradition, North American New Rhetoric, and the Australian Systemic-Functional School, providing the reader with an understanding of how these different schools of thought can work together to advance our knowledge of genre. The international perspective illustrates that much of the work being done outside the United States, while not always groundbreaking or in conversation with current theory, is yet consistently interesting and theoretically sound, often approaching the study of genre in new and creative ways.

The book is broken into five parts: "Advances in Genre Theories," "Genre and the Professions," "Genre and Media," "Genre in Teaching and Learning," and "Genre in Writing Across the Curriculum." The first section, "Advances in Genre Theories," consists of the essays that seem to push the hardest at developing new ways of looking at genre. For example, in "World of Genre – Metaphors of Genre," John M. Swales argues that useful metaphors for genres may be "genre-as-institution" and "genre-as-species," as such metaphors help us to trace genres from their inception to their variations and sometimes demise. Paul Prior argues in "From Speech Genres to Mediated Multimodal Genres Systems: Bakhtin, Voloshinov, and the Question of Writing" that Bakhtin's understanding of genres as composed utterances as being equivalent to spoken utterances fails to take into account the writing process. And Favio Jose Rauen's "Relevance and Genre: Theoretical and Conceptual Interfaces" combines relevance theory with genre theory by questioning how relevance limits genres.

With Swales on one hand arguing that genre analysis is meant to track "textual regularities and irregularities and explain them in terms of the relevant and pertinent social circumstances and the rhetorical demands they engender" (14) and Coutinho and Miranda on the other hand arguing for new ways of analyzing genres, I was hoping that more of the chapters devoted to genre analyses would push their discussion sections further, and I was left wanting to see how each analysis contributed to a larger perspective of genre. Often, the conclusions felt a bit abrupt. For example, in the second section, Leonardo Mozdzenski argues in "The Sociohistorical Constitution of the Genre *Legal Booklet*: A Critical Approach" that legal booklets are influenced by religious and school primers, by political pamphlets, and by educational booklets produced in Brazil. After an extensive genre analysis, he concludes that legal booklets use strategies common to these antecedent genres. "The Organization and Functions of the Press *Dossier*: The Case of Media Discourse on the Environment in Portugal," Rui Ramos's contribution in the third section, offers a detailed textual analysis of this document but then concludes in one brief paragraph that the document has a circular organization. And Giovanni Parodi's "Written Genres in University Studies: Evidence from an Academic Corpus of Spanish in Four Disciplines," in which he explains an ongoing project that involves the collection and analysis of academic and professional texts from different disciplines, makes assumptions based on unbalanced evidence and ends by suggesting that something should be done with all of the data. These few genre analyses are fairly representative of a large portion of the chapters, and while I appreciate the international perspective, such selections could benefit from more discussion. In particular, I had hoped to see how such analyses might contribute to our understanding of either the people who use that genre or the community in which that genre functions. Perhaps because scholarship on genre theory has a longer history in the United States than in many other places, scholars in other countries are still working to develop their own theories and to explore the many creative approaches to the study of genres. This development is especially prevalent in Brazil, and one selection from this text that succeeds in using genre analysis to make a larger argument is Débora de Carvalho Figueiredo's "Narrative and Identity Formation: An Analysis of Media Personal Accounts from Patients of Cosmetic Plastic Surgery." She argues that choosing to have plastic surgery requires a patient to "uptake" a specific way of being and adhere to a certain narrative, and while she analyzes the personal accounts in detail, she also uses this analysis to make a valid argument about how genres can require people who use them to adhere to a certain identity.

Other selections within this book also work to provide new insights. I would argue that the strongest section is "Genre in Teaching and Learning," which offers us six selections from scholars with a variety of backgrounds. Bazerman's piece begins this section, as he argues in "Genre and Cognitive Development: Beyond Writing to Learn" that the challenges that come with attempting new genres may help with cognitive growth, as "genres identify a problem space for the developing writer to work in" (291). Also in this section is Amy Devitt's "Teaching Critical Genre Awareness," an engaging piece that takes a slightly different pedagogical perspective than her 2004 co-authored textbook *Scenes of Writing: Strategies for Composing with Genres*. Devitt uses tagmemics here, arguing that we can teach genres as particles/things, as waves/processes, or as fields/contexts, as each represents a pedagogical application derived from current and sometimes competing theories that debate if and how genres can be taught.

Other especially notable pieces in this book are scattered throughout the remaining sections. In "Stories of Becoming: A Study of Novice Engineers Learning Genres of their Profession," Natasha Artemeva follows four students from an Engineering communication class to their workplace, noting that "genre knowledge ingredients" – including agency, content expertise, and cultural capital – are necessary to help students learn genres of their professions. Anthony Paré, Doreen Starke-Meyerring, and Lynn McAlpine's "The Dissertation as Multi-Genre: Many Readers, Many Readings" looks at five different types of readers for dissertations, concluding that the dissertation functions as a multi-genre. And "Exploring Notions of Genre in 'Academic Literacies' and 'Writing Across the Curriculum': Approaches Across Countries and Contexts," by David Russell et al., provides a detailed comparison of Writing Across the Curriculum programs in the United States with Academic Literacies, a newer writing-intensive program in England. One call at the end of their chapter argues for collaboration with secondary schools and with second-language learning communities.

What struck me about this book as a whole was that many authors drew from the same body of knowledge in their works, especially Carolyn Miller's "Genre as Social Action," Bakhtin's "The Problem of Speech Genres," Swales's *Genre Analysis: English in Academic and Research Settings,* or a selection from the corpus of work done by Bazerman and Russell. While I would like to have seen more current works on genre theory being put into conversation with one another, I also appreciate that such landmark pieces on genre theory were used both to frame a variety of perspectives and to illustrate the international and intercultural power of genres. The editors argue that "forging effective genres is a matter of global well-being" (xiv), and this book, the collaboration of a plurality of voices, is an important step in the right direction. Further, this edited collection is timely given that the next SIGET conference will occur in Summer 2011, and I am optimistic that scholars will challenge themselves to advance our theories of genre, perhaps by studying how genres can help us to understand communication problems on an international level or by researching ways to enable people who find themselves disempowered by genres. Overall, I would recommend this book as an important read, especially for those who are interested in the current state of developments in genre theory from a global perspective.

Blacksburg, VA

Works Cited

Bakhtin, Mikhail M. "The Problem of Speech Genres." *Speech Genres and Other Late Essays.* Trans. Vern W. McGee. Ed. Caryl Emerson and Michael Holquist. Austin: U of Texas P, 1986. 60-102. Print.

Bazerman, Charles. "The Life of Genre, the Life in the Classroom." *Genre and Writ-*

ing. Ed. Wendy Bishop and Hans Ostrum. Portsmouth: Boynton/Cook, 1997. 19-26. Print.

Devitt, Amy, Mary Jo Reiff, and Anis Bawarshi. *Scenes of Writing: Strategies for Composing with Genres*. New York: Longman, 2004. Print.

Miller, Carolyn. "Genre as Social Action. *Quarterly Journal of Speech* 70 (1984): 151-167. Print.

Swales, John M. *Genre Analysis: English in Academic and Research Settings*. Cambridge: Cambridge UP, 1990. Print.

Copyright Clarity: How Fair Use Supports Digital Learning, by Renee Hobbs. Thousand Oaks: Corwin & NCTE, 2010. 128 pp.

Reviewed by Kerrie L. Carsey, Miami University

Last Fall, one of my first-year writing students devoted much of his research and writing to examining The DOW Chemical Company. "Paul" wrote a rhetorical analysis of a DOW's television ad in their "Human Element" campaign. Then, he wrote a persuasive essay, calling consumers to hold the company accountable for some of its questionable corporate practices in Third World countries. Finally, Paul blended content from these alphabetic texts into a multimodal project. The first segment of his video contained an excerpt from a DOW ad, a visual feast of images such as mountain landscapes and close-ups of children of various races and cultures. The narrator explained that even more valuable than the elements on the periodic table, the "human element"—curiosity and ingenuity—could improve the lives of people across the globe. Then, Paul's voice intervened, asking if DOW was living up to this ideal. As he spoke about chemical spills and the use of FDA-banned chemicals in overseas facilities, the viewer saw video and photographs of disaster victims and babies with birth defects. As Paul explained DOW's perfecting of napalm during the Vietnam War, he showed a clip from the film "We Were Soldiers," with Vietnamese and American fighters falling in slow-motion explosions of fire.

Obviously, Paul, like many of his classmates, made use of copyrighted material, and we had to address questions of infringement and fair use. Were he to post his project to YouTube, would take-down notices spell its end? Might he receive cease and desist letters from DOW, from the photographers or their publishers, or from Paramount Pictures? And would those actions and threats be legally justified? Many students wondered if they should keep their projects to themselves or perhaps take advantage of YouTube's privacy settings, protecting their videos from searches and allowing only those who possessed the link to view their work.

In *Copyright Clarity: How Fair Use Supports Digital Learning*, Renee Hobbs works to dispel "copyfright," this wariness, on the part of students and instructors across disciplines, surrounding the use and sharing of copyrighted material. Hobbs, a media literacy education specialist, develops curriculum materials for K-12 educators. However, as a professor at Temple University, her research often includes the voices of university instructors. In this concise text, Hobbs succeeds at addressing a wide range of educators, and anyone training educators, who wish to compose and teach with copyrighted material. Appendices contain excerpts of copyright law and materials for staff development workshops on copyright and fair use. Her inclusion of early education classroom practice sets this work apart from, say, the September 2010 special issue of *Computers and Composition*, devoted to cultural contexts of copyright. But *Copyright Clarity* offers a valuable and informed perspective in this important conversation.

Hobbs operates on the premise that "appropriation is a powerful instructional tool for student learning" (6), that the reworking of borrowed material promotes creativity and creates knowledge. Chapter 1 asserts that students are already consuming large quantities of media messages through television, social networking, video games, movies, and music. Effective teaching draws students to evaluate and analyze these messages, creating media literacy and opening the door for them to produce information. For instance, by bringing clips from a popular sitcom into the classroom, teachers can foster discussion and writing about depictions of women in the media. However, much of this material is protected by copyright, and teachers often fall victim to misinformation, seeing only the ways copyright law protects owners and failing to take advantage of users' rights.

Complicating matters is the flexibility, sometimes ambiguity, of copyright law, which is designed to adapt to changing contexts and technologies. Hobbs insists that these laws cannot be reduced to simple checklists. Rather, users must think, examining each situation to make reasonable fair use determinations. If responsible fair use of copyrighted material is locked behind misinformation and confusion, the key to informed fair use determinations is "transformativeness," a creative repurposing of copyrighted material (8). This concept acts as a barometer, indicating when our cutting-and-pasting amounts to theft, and when it contributes to knowledge production.

Chapter 2, "Dispelling Copyright Confusion," provides concise definitions of copyright, fair use, public domain, and intellectual property. Hobbs frames the issue by offering three stakeholders: creators, publishers, and users/consumers. Copyright protects the creators and producers of material. However, Hobbs shows that the Founding Fathers intended copyright to encourage the spread of knowledge, in that it "promote[s] the progress of science and useful arts, by securing for limited times" the exclusive right to writings and inventions (18). In other words, the ability to keep exclusive rights motivates creators toward discovery.

Fair use protects users of copyrighted material, acting as a safety valve to prevent the complete control of information, which would otherwise amount to a form of private censorship. Hobbs provides helpful text boxes throughout the book, including a citation of Section 107 of the Fair Use Doctrine. To reproduce copyrighted work for "purposes such as criticism, comment, news reporting, teaching (including multiple copies for classroom use), scholarship, or research" constitutes fair use and is not copyright infringement (qtd. in Hobbs 19). But in addition to these allowances, users must consider the purpose, nature, amount used, and market impact when working with copyrighted material. Again, transformativeness is essential to juggling these considerations, and users must discern whether they have sufficiently repurposed the material or whether they have simply copied in such a way that competes with the owner or deprives him/her of profit.

However, FBI warnings, cease-and-desist letters, and file-sharing litigation can obscure this balance of rights and contribute to a "climate of uncertainty and fear" (21). Confusion hinders the spread of innovation, both in instructional practices and in the resulting student work. Hobbs is careful to point out that even educational-use guidelines, provided by institutions, are not law, and that educators should not trust simple lists, charts, or graphs that specify exactly what users may or may not do. These guidelines are often written by lawyers who seek to narrow or oversimplify what is a flexible law. Many seemingly official policy guidelines do not even address fair use and often equate sharing with stealing (35).

In chapter 3, Hobbs continues to push readers to think critically and make an informed fair use determination. She provides real student assignments, such as a slide show that compares and contrasts two influential photographers. Of course, this task would require students to use copyrighted images. Hobbs asserts the contextually situated criterion, "What has the student done with this material?" (41), using transformativeness as a standard. In other words, has the student added value and repurposed the work? Considering other layers of fair use law, such as purposes of "comment" and "research," adds confidence to these determinations.

By chapter 4, I sensed my increased comfort level with making these critical choices. True to her belief about the need to contextualize every use of copyrighted material, Hobbs refuses to draw concrete lines, such as the exact situation in which to seek permission and pay appropriate fees. Although I would not say she completely "dispels" confusion, she does put the reader at ease that with an informed and good faith determination, teachers and students need not fear entanglement with copyright law.

The final chapter explores the uncertain future of copyright and fair use. Hobbs outlines possible avenues, such as a more robust creative commons licensure system and "some rights reserved" law (90). But she has been so successful at holding to the balance of respect for owners and users, the reader immediately sees how these scenarios might infringe upon some stakeholders' rights. In other words, the route Hobbs has been advocating, that of critical thought leading to informed fair use determinations under existing law, seems most palatable.

As the above chapter summaries suggest, Hobbs tends to merge the practices of viewing reproduced material and composing with that material under the blanket term "use." As a college composition instructor, I would have appreciated more singular attention to digital writing with copyrighted texts. However, copyright law supports Hobbs's conflation. Further, this move allows her to maintain her broad (K-12 and beyond) audience. In fact, for post-secondary educators, I recommend pairing Hobbs' book with Martine Courant Rife's chapter, "Ideas Toward a Fair Use Heuristic" in the 2009 collection *Composition and Copyright*. In tandem, these texts outline current issues surrounding copyright law and offer not easy answers, but thought-provoking steps toward a heuristic for teachers, one that promotes "digital citizenship" in the classroom (Hobbs 94).

Thanks to this text, Paul and I felt confident that he had aptly repurposed the feature film, directing that material away from its primary original purposes (entertainment and expression) and toward a new objective—critique of the corporation that developed and supplied napalm. Further, we decided his goals of criticism, comment, and research protected his inclusion of the DOW ad and other visual images. Soon, Paul and I will meet to discuss publication in the form of submission to a department writing award. He plans to share his work with confidence.

Oxford, OH

Works Cited

Rife, Martine Courant. "Ideas Toward a Fair Use Heuristic." *Composition and Copyright*. Ed. Steve Westbrook. Albany: SUNY P, 2009. Print.

Decolonizing Literacy: Mexican Lives in the Era of Global Capitalism, by Gregorio Hernandez-Zamora. Bristol: Multilingual Matters, 2010. 223 pp.

Reviewed by Rebecca Lorimer, University of Wisconsin-Madison

Multilingual Matters publishes books that continue to challenge understandings of global language movement and power in its series Critical

Language and Literacy Studies. Gregorio Hernandez-Zamora's study of the literacy histories of marginalized Mexicans in Mexico City and the U.S. represents the best of the series as it describes seven individuals appropriating and resisting dominant literacy practices in neocolonial settings. Hernandez-Zamora's work is truly critical, both in its politically-radical edge and its critique of literacy development programs, cultural relativism, and scholarship that is ever-coining new terms to describe the messy process of language and literacy learning. Composition Studies should feel both inspired and indicted by this book. Our research occasionally depends on prefixes (bi, multi, trans) to describe complexity in writing without attending to the social and historical systems from which writing practices come; our teaching sometimes uses this research to make choices about curriculum or assessment. *Decolonizing Literacy* shows writing researchers and teachers how to slow down and reconsider what literacy is for.

In the three parts of the book, a theoretical introduction, a set of case studies, and closing implications, Hernandez-Zamora embeds lived experiences of literacy in long histories of colonialism, arguing that citizenship as "self-making and being-made within webs of power" is a necessary condition for the development of literacy, rather than an outcome of it (42). Hernandez-Zamora supports this provocative claim first by grounding the case studies in an ongoing story of imperialism and neocolonial economic exclusion, and then by developing individual voices from this historical space, including reflections of satisfaction as well as struggle and loss. It is this insistence on contradiction and resistance to romanticism that is the real contribution of the book—Hernandez-Zamora is not painting a rosy picture here, but his frank analysis of subjugated writers is an important reminder that active and creative uses of literacy are essential to establishing a sense of self.

In part 1, Hernandez-Zamora lays out a theoretical context based in postcolonialism, Freirean tenets of critical consciousness, Moll and Greenberg's funds of knowledge approach, and new literacy studies' belief in literacy as historical, social, and cultural practice rather than individual cognitive skill. But Hernandez-Zamora pushes beyond this theoretical groundwork, noting, for example, that marginalized writers' funds of knowledge include constraints as well as possibilities, and that learning the language of one's colonizers can involve an appropriation of unwelcome linguistic histories. The section culminates in a critique of international literacy programs that prescribe literacy as economic medicine, asserting above all that "postcolonial subjects *have ideas of their own*" about what literacy can or can't do in their lives (21).

Part 2, the longest of the book, is divided into chapters of case studies as "agents," "transnationals," and "survivors." The cases are representative of a large group of in-depth life-history interviews carried out by Hernandez-Zamora over an eight-year span with individuals living in the *colonias* of

Mexico City and in poor neighborhoods of Nashville, Charlotte, and California's Bay Area. For Hernandez-Zamora, "agents" are those who have successfully appropriated literacy as a means to self-author their experience of freedom and citizenship in impoverished areas of Mexico. "Transnationals" are cases of Mexican immigrants living in the U.S. who describe themselves as "citizens of nowhere," neither of dominant Mexican institutions from which they feel excluded or powerful U.S. systems in which they can't legally participate (40). The "survivors" are cases whose literate knowledge and education cannot compete with the powerful social and economic forces keeping them in place in Mexico.

In each chapter the voice of the case study is generously featured—Hernandez-Zamora lets the cases speak for themselves about their appropriation of, and sometimes self-exclusion from, dominant literacy practices. After each case description, Hernandez-Zamora analyzes patterns of "access" to and "appropriation" of literacy practices, looking especially for identity and literacy development. He is purposeful in his recovery of previously-silent voices often missed by large programmatic surveys or standardized literacy tests. In this way, *Decolonizing Literacy* is peopled by individual lives rather than static linguistic data so that readers can, as Hernandez-Zamora says, "meet History in person" (23). A brief comparison of just two of these cases will demonstrate both the book's range of described lives and its argument that self-determination and self-authorship is needed first for literacy development.

In chapter 3, Saul, an "agent," appropriates reading and writing practices to self-author his own life experience. Hernandez-Zamora describes Saul reading and discussing current news stories with his wife Chela, as well as reading religious and non-religious texts with their sociopolitically-minded religious study group. In his mid-sixties at the time of the interview, Saul had only three years of schooling, but a vast repertoire of literacy practices, acting as a literacy broker for his community, writing petition letters for neighborhood causes, and leading a life-story-telling group with elderly neighbors. Hernandez-Zamora explains that this literacy development was "crucially fueled by [Saul's] engagement in workplaces, community organizations and social movements which offered sophisticated, powerful and critical knowledge and discourse practices often unavailable in standard adult education" (68). In this way, Saul's case is a success story, depicting an individual whose position in his community and belief in his ability to effect change allowed him to build literacy practices outside of any literacy program or school curriculum.

In chapter 4, however, Laura, a "transnational," is shown to both appropriate and exclude herself from dominant literacy practices, especially in English. Laura, who crossed illegally into the U.S. with her two children to join her husband, worked in packing plants, hotels, and at McDonald's, settings in which she learned lessons in both English as well as American racism. Laura says she dreamed of the American life she saw on TV in Mexico, but found herself unable to access that life as a non-citizen of the U.S. While immigration helped Laura and her family attain a more secure level of material well-being, Laura believes that no amount of English or writing experience will make them full participants in U.S. life. In other words, while Laura is the most proficient in English of Hernandez-Zamora's cases, she is also the most reticent to believe that such literate skill matters. Describing her sons, Laura says she "[cuts] their wings before they start flying" so that they don't dream of a future life that doesn't exist for them in the U.S. or in Mexico (109). Here Hernandez-Zamora shows that Laura's literacy, learned in contexts of racism and rote work rather than community and civic engagement, will not develop to facilitate feelings of control over or freedom in her life.

The book ends with part 3, in which Hernandez-Zamora analyzes current learning and literacy theories that silence non-dominant groups and those that encourage writing and thinking for more full experiences of citizenship. In particular, he challenges skills-based literacy education, saying such programs overlook the "deprived socioeconomic conditions in which individual lives are based" and inhibit the "*desires* and *possibilities* for intellectual, literacy, and social growth" (7). Throughout *Decolonizing Literacy* Hernandez-Zamora argues that these possibilities are actually created through community-based groups and movements, those based in spiritualism, community activism, unionism, or even online escapism, not schools.

The book's focus on sociohistorical conditions rather than literacy pedagogy might leave readers feeling powerless. Without concrete suggestions or plans, teachers and researchers working inside the educational institutions Hernandez-Zamora critiques might be tempted to shrug away responsibility—who are we to blame the very institutions that pay us, some may ask. Hernandez-Zamora, however, is not a fatalist. He does not let readers off the hook by suggesting that social and economic forces overpower the individuals working within them. Instead, he proposes that educators search for learning theories that move writers from passivity to activity and from silence to voice. He hopes teachers will resist the temptation to provide poor people with quiet skills, and focus first on "empowering people to transform themselves, their communities and the larger society" (197). In the final chapter, Hernandez-Zamora also offers models of grassroots-based organizations that use a functional rather than skills-based approach to literacy, in which literacy and education are not ends in themselves but aspects of larger projects that address systems of inequality. Strangely, Hernandez-Zamora's use of "functional" in part 3 is rather at odds with his clear critique of the term in part 1.

Decolonizing Literacy begins and ends with history, foregrounding an ongoing social narrative of exclusion as the real issue for literacy education. In this way, the book is at its best a reminder that "old" literacies, those that predate digital, multi-, or trans- literacies, still exist in postcolonial contexts, even as "new" literacies take center stage in composition research and teaching. *Decolonizing Literacy* reminds us most of all to treat our students, especially those from impoverished or postcolonial backgrounds, not as blank slates who walk into our classrooms but as ongoing historical stories that can be supported through writing.

Madison, WI

Engaging Audience: Writing in an Age of New Literacies, edited by M. Elizabeth Weiser, Brian M. Fehler, and Angela M. González. Urbana: NCTE, 2009. 340 pp.

Reviewed by Matthew Ortoleva, Johnson & Wales University

Engaging Audience: Writing in an Age of New Litericies, a new collection of sixteen essays edited by M. Elizabeth Weiser, Brian M. Fehler, and Angela M. González, considers the rhetorical concept of audience in the twenty-first century. The foundation of this collection is Lisa Ede and Andrea Lunsford's seminal work on audience as first encapsulated in their 1984 *CCC* article, "Audience Addressed/Audience Invoked: The Role of Audience in Composition Theory and Pedagogy," which is reprinted in this collection. The concept of AA/AI, as it is often referred to in this collection, flows through these essays "in the manner of a leaf following a current, swirling into side currents, turning in eddies, then flowing on," to borrow a metaphor from the editors (xii). Each essay in this collection expands on the questions that Ede and Lunsford ask to begin "Audience Addressed/Audience Invoked": "How can we best define the audience of a written discourse? What does it mean to address an audience? To what degree should teachers stress audience in their assignments and discussions? What is the best way to help students recognize the significance of this critical element in any rhetorical situation?" (3). The contributors of this collection—including Ede and Lunsford, who contribute a new article on the subject—ask these questions at a time when the need to understand the new literacies emerging from twenty-first-century digital environments is drastically expanding.

This collection is organized into three sections, the first of which is "The Audience Stream: Following the Current of Audience Theory." This first section is devoted solely to Ede and Lunsford with their original article of AA/AI starting the collection followed by the reprinting of their 1996 re-engagement with the concept of AA/AI in "Representing Audience: 'Successful' Discourse and Disciplinary Critique," which also first appeared in *CCC*. The third essay of the "Audience Stream" section, and perhaps the most notable of the collection, is Ede and Lunsford's newest engagement with AA/AI, an article written for this collection entitled "Among the Audience: On Audience in an Age of New Literacies." In "Among the Audience" Ede and Lunsford consider how twenty-first-century literacies and participatory media challenge older notions of authorship and audience, and call into question the usefulness of AA/AI in new communication environments where the roles of writers and audiences destabilize and frequently shift. Ede and Lunsford convincingly argue that the dialogic relationship of AA/AI still make it a productive construct to understand the new literacies and participatory communicative practices found in the new digital environments. Ultimately, Ede and Lunsford do recognize that although AA/AI is useful in helping understand the complexity of all forms of communication, "understanding the complexity of the writing process, audience awareness, and participation calls for more specific grounded, and nuanced analysis than the binary of addressed and invoked audiences can provide" (56). As such, to more fully understand the complexities of audience, they call for deeper analysis of concrete situations that ethnographic and other qualitative studies might provide. Moreover, Ede and Lunsford recognize that understanding these new literacies calls for a convergence of two previous separate strands of scholarship: audience and collaboration. Ede and Lunsford conclude their essay by stressing the importance of teaching the concept of audience and how it relates to the ethical implications of being engaged in acts of participatory communication. Ede and Lunsford suggest that although students may be digital natives, they still need to become aware of the types of audiences they might encounter when they write, how they might negotiate these audiences effectively and responsibly, and how they might "build bridges between the seemingly private voices they inhabit on-line and the public ones they can establish" (63).

The second section of this collection, entitled "Theory Streams: Ebbs and Flows of Audience through Composition and Communication," contains two essays. Traci Zimmerman's "Authors, Audiences, and The Gaps Between" examines audience through theories of authorship, including those of Foucault and Barthes, and calls on us to teach in the gaps between author and audience, and between writers and readers. David Beard's "Communicating with Audience," embraces the interdisciplinary character of this collection and reaches into two fields often neglected by Rhetoric and Composition—the fields of interpersonal and mass communication, where the concept of audience is often studied empirically—to understand audience activity and how audiences consume texts. Both essays in this section make fine contributions to the collection and are both equally engaging. Still, of the three sections of the collection, "Theory Streams" feels somewhat anemic. Zimmerman's and Beard's articles form a strong basis for engaging AA/AI; however, missed is an opportunity to put Ede and Lunsford's work into deeper conversation with other theories of audience, such as James Porter's concept of the discourse community or Kenneth Burke's theory of identification, both mentioned in other sections of the collection but fall short of a deeper theoretical engagement with AA/AI.

The third section, "Praxis Streams: Audience Wending through Classrooms and Communities," makes up the bulk of this collection with eleven essays. This section is rich with concrete examples of how teachers from a variety of sub-disciplines within Rhetoric and Composition, and some disciplines outside of Rhetoric and Composition, teach the concept of audience. David Dayton's article "New Media Personas and Scenarios" describes his use of personas and scenarios, which are "visual-verbal representations of key audience groups" (115) and "bring imagination and intuition more forcefully into our analysis and invention of audiences" (127). Dayton's article is particularly useful and includes a sample persona created by one of his students, as well as a brief history of the way personas and scenarios have been used by design teams in workplace writing environments. Inadvertently perhaps, Dayton's article also hints at intersections with creative writing pedagogy, as students, through the creation of these personas and scenarios, become storytellers. Bob Batchelor's "Tactician and Strategist" turns to the field of public relations, where audience considerations are at the center of all writing tasks. In "I Can Take a Stance," Tom Pace embraces Peter Elbow's idea of first ignoring audience to focus on topics and ideas, so later when a writer chooses to no longer ignore audience and rather to let audience considerations shape the text, he or she may find a new purpose for revision. Marie Paretti, in "When the Teacher Is the Audience," considers the intersection of activity theory and genre theory as a way to understand how texts mediate the relationship between writer and audience while also examining the problems created by bifurcated activity systems produced by the always present teacher-as-audience conundrum. Paretti offers an example of how she addresses this problem through a memo assignment which explicitly makes her the audience and offers a site for a real exchange of information, information that Paretti uses as a program administrator. In "The Self-Addressed Stamped Envelope," Alexandria Peary also calls on activity theory as a way of engaging students in the concept of audience. For Peary, activity theory serves to demonstrate how students might grasp a practical understanding of audience by interacting with editors in a writing-for-publication course.

Phyllis Mentzell Ryder's chapter turns to public writing and pedagogies of service learning to explain the work of "public-making," while Sharon McKenzie Stevens turns to translation studies to demonstrate the complexity and the ethical complications that surface in collaborative acts of writing as she argues for the need for pedagogies that help students address different, more-powerful audiences without necessarily "assimilating to audience expectations" (232). Traci Freeman's chapter "Can I get a Witness? Faith-Based Reasoning and The Academic Audience" examines the challenges of teaching audience to students who turn to faith-based reasoning and religious rhetoric and how such a turn may disrupt notions of academic audiences. Those who teach in communities where expressions of faith are not so overt may find this article unexpectedly engaging. Freeman argues for the need to move beyond merely suggesting to students that faith-based arguments are ineffective in the academic discourse community and rather to reconsider the often provincial view of academic audience. Freeman offers an example of how she uses stasis and a personal essay assignment to allow students of faith to interrogate the commonplace notion that faith-based arguments are not welcome by academic audiences. In "Theorizing Audience in Web-Based Self-Presentation" Erin Karper calls on Kenneth Burke's theory of identification as a means of understanding the interactive nature of audience in digital environments, and in "Reading Audiences" Dan Keller turns to reading pedagogies to examine how students' understanding of audiences are shaped by their reading practices. Finally, in "Writing Assessment as New Literacy," Lee Nickoson-Massey considers how classroom writing assessment practices and peer-response activities are rich areas of inquiry into the concept of audience.

This timely collection clearly demonstrates that the concept of audience and the struggles on how to help students understand this important rhetorical concept is alive and well in our field. This collection also serves to remind us that the theories and concepts that define our field of study are shifting, evolving, and often lead us in exciting new directions.

Providence, RI

Democracies to Come: Rhetorical Action, Neoliberalism, and Communities of Resistance, by Rachel Riedner and Kevin Mahoney. Lanham: Lexington, 2008. 142 pp.

Reviewed by Rebecca Richards, University of Arizona

Trying to translate the principles of critical pedagogy into the U.S. composition classroom has not been without challenges. U.S. composition instructors drawn to Freire's work, in particular, have had to attend to the differences and privileges of their specific geopolitical location from that in which Freire wrote and worked. In addition, U.S. composition instructors must also confront the tension presented in the U.S. media, which quickly and superficially proclaims that U.S citizens live in an already-free and egalitarian society, all while lived experiences and observations tell us otherwise. In *Democracies to Come: Rhetorical Action, Neoliberalism, and Communities of Resistance,* Riedner and Mahoney situate critical pedagogy in conversation with elements of participatory democratic action, which is no easy task in today's globalized society. Instead of narrowly defining pedagogy as a theory that informs classroom praxis, the writers define pedagogy as the theory that underlines "lived political work" (11). After introducing the major themes of the book in the first chapter, each subsequent chapter looks at highly divergent rhetorical situations to demonstrate the ways in which instructors can use critical pedagogy to interrupt hegemonic practices. Chapters 2 through 6 employ Riedner and Mahoney's broader definition of pedagogy to help composition instructors think about how our actions and commitments—both inside and outside the classroom—enact methods of critical pedagogy, and the selected case studies provide interesting portraits of what critical pedagogy can look like for composition instructors.

To open and frame the analyses in the rest of the chapters, Riedner and Mahoney's first chapter addresses the tension of the self-proclaimed freedom of the U.S. democracy and the reality of lived experience by asking readers to remember Derrida's proclamation that "democracy remains to come." For Riedner and Mahoney, this phrase explains the contradiction in celebratory nationalistic messages and hegemonic practices. *Democracies to Come*, as a book, reminds its readers that democracy is an ideal that a society must continually struggle to enact, and that pedagogy is the vehicle for moving toward that ideal. The first chapter pays particular attention to the notion of *kairos*, looking at how individuals must attend to the urgency and shifting nature of agency in each rhetorical exigency. In doing so, Riedner and Mahoney encourage composition instructors to consider how their own local situation gives them unique access to intervene in neoliberal logic with progressive rhetorical actions, which then frames the subsequent chapters where they investigate locations of interruption.

In chapter 2, the writers trace the emergence and circulation of the logic of neoliberalism, which they define as more than just an economic concept of the upward distribution of wealth. The writers argue that it is also a rhetoric and a pedagogy that forestalls action and limits possibilities because neoliberalism configures the "relationship of power and between labor and capital, consolidates identities, interpellates bodies into systems of identity, and creates relationships across public and private spheres, it creates deep and even violent economic, political, and cultural ruptures"

(21). Riedner and Mahoney maintain that neoliberalism is the broad and abstract logic that critical pedagogy seeks to interrupt. However, even though Composition Studies continually takes up critical pedagogy as the means for liberatory action, such work often times creates unintended byproducts—ones that reproduce neoliberal logic. Students and instructors alike can experience despair, passivity, and apathy as they uncover some of the invisible mechanisms and flows of power—especially those found in the processes of globalization, such as inhumane labor practices and gendered inequity. The writers are keenly aware of the difficulties of enacting critical pedagogy in neoliberal spaces, which is an asset of the book—they understand the limitations of educational practices and spaces. Particularly, they are attentive to the identity crisis of higher education, which has become more and more of a corporatized space where students receive commodities, e.g., diplomas, and where academic labor is quantified through publications. While the book thoroughly critiques the marketplace logic of the university, the writers remain hopeful that academic spaces exist that allow for new literacies that can intervene in these dominant discourses.

Following the critique of neoliberalism and the university in chapter 2, Riedner and Mahoney look to specific spaces that can provide interruptions to neoliberal rhetorical habits. In chapter 3, for example, the writers claim that the university campus can be a space to interrupt neoliberalism. In this chapter, the rhetorical action they analyze is a sit-in at the George Washington University student center—a demonstration to support adjunct faculty and support service workers, for which students were arrested and yet the student leading the protest was awarded during the graduation ceremony. In the discussions (or lack thereof) that followed the student-organized sit-in, Riedner and Mahoney demonstrate how coercion functions at the university community, where interruption is rewarded symbolically but it is also met with police discipline and not engaged rhetorically.

While chapter 3 looks at university spaces beyond the classroom, chapters 4 and 5 engage the classroom as a site of production of neoliberal despair and benevolence. Both Riedner and Mahoney share with readers their experience of teaching students about transnational power relations in their classrooms at George Washington and Kutztown University, respectively. Riedner's experience of teaching "Women in the Global Economy" led students to replicating a rhetoric of benevolence—a key component of neoliberal logic as "benevolence gives neoliberal authority as a feeling and self-identification" (55). But that feeling *is* a kairotic site for intervention where we can ask students to develop an understanding of social relationships that do not rely on subordination. Likewise, Mahoney's teaching experience demonstrates how the authentic moral outrage of coming into a new understanding of how the world works can often and invisibly turn into despair through personal "rational deliberation" that disassociates emotion from knowledge. What is productive about both of these examples is that the authors are attentive to the importance of emotion in rhetorical action as well as the urgency in placing these discourses of despair and benevolence into larger communicative networks. What this means for composition instructors is speaking to these emotions aloud (either in class discussion or writing) is important work since, most often, these emotions are processed individually and internally. Both benevolence and despair are collective neoliberal experiences, which means that there is the potential for organizing rhetorical action around them. Riedner and Mahoney point out that walking away from these moments in exasperation, as we all have, would miss out on the deeply kairotic moments for critical pedagogy.

Finally, the last chapter addresses specific writing practices that hold the potential to produce alternative social realities. Zapatista writing voices opposition to the Mexican government through the rhetorical strategies of irrationality, silliness, and laughter. The authors show how these strategies transgress the authoritative rhetoric of the government while acting upon the shared emotions of the writer and audience. The authors are careful in situating Zapatista writing in conjunction with academic writing, noting that doing so can flatten the context of the political discourse. In no way do Riedner and Mahoney implicate academic writing as equal to the political struggle confronted in Zapatista writing. However some cultural studies scholarship shares with Zapatista writing the ability to thwart neoliberal hegemonic practices through writing strategies. Academics can be transgressive or resistant to dominant neoliberal logic by creating works that "*produce*. . . beyond the scope of capital's control" (103). This means that not all academic writing—not even in the field of Composition Studies—must be accountable to the corporate publications culture that demands that research *do* something other than critique. Neoliberalism critiques such academic writing as elitist and irrelevant since it does not contribute to the expansion of the market. But feminist cultural studies, e.g. the work of Judith Butler, deliberately resists such a narrow definition of "relevant." Riedner and Mahoney argue that we need to continue this type of work to expose the "excess, gaps, differences, and openings" in neoliberal rhetoric (103).

Democracies to Come does an excellent job defining and explaining how rhetorical action intervenes into neoliberal politics both inside and outside of the classroom, making it a good read for composition teachers who engage in service learning, participatory action research, or critical pedagogy. It is an important addition to composition scholarship in critical pedagogy and social action in that it is concerned with how neoliberalism, when left unchecked, can forestall even the best intentions for social justice.

Additionally, Riedner and Mahoney are attentive to the role that emotion plays in perpetuating hegemony as well as in creating potentials for action; they do not easily resolve the simultaneous function of emotion as emancipatory or unproductive. Instead, they provide the readers with concrete and tangible examples that are messy and contradictory, much like the daily experience in the composition classroom. *Democracies to Come* kicks off a series from Lexington Press on Cultural Studies, Pedagogy, and Activism; therefore readers can anticipate an ongoing conversation of the topics addressed in this book.

Tucson, AZ

Organic Writing Assessment: Dynamic Criteria Mapping in Action, by Bob Broad, Linda Adler-Kassner, Barry Alford, Jane Detweiler, Heidi Estrem, Susanmarie Harrington, Maureen McBride, Eric Stalions, and Scott Weeden. Logan: Utah State UP, 2009. 174 pp.

Reviewed by Janet S. Zepernick, Pittsburg State University

Organic Writing Assessment: Dynamic Criteria Mapping in Action continues the work begun by Bob Broad in an earlier volume, *What We Really Value: Beyond Rubrics in Teaching and Assessing*, where Broad introduces dynamic criteria mapping (DCM) as both a philosophy of and approach to writing assessment. The current volume opens with an introduction in which Broad summarizes the philosophy of DCM (but not the methodology; see *What We Really Value* for a procedural explanation). Each of the five subsequent chapters describes a large-scale assessment project undertaken using DCM: Linda Adler-Kassner and Heidi Estrem's assessment of the first-year writing program at Eastern Michigan University; Barry Alford's development of shared learning outcomes for all of Mid Michigan Community College's course offerings; Jane Detweiler and Maureen McBride's evaluation of writing and critical thinking in the core writing course at University of Nevada, Reno; Susanmarie Harrington and Scott Weeden's work to develop new program goals in the required writing program at Indiana University-Purdue University Indianapolis; and Eric Stalions's validation test of the first-year writing placement process at Bowling Green State University.

Philosophically, DCM privileges local control in every aspect of the assessment process, celebrates the complexity and diversity of features that might represent "good writing" in any given context, and honors the rhetorical process of negotiating local writing values. DCM's imperative that process should emerge from context requires that each institution develop a unique, local methodology, and the five projects represented in this collection do follow very different paths. Beneath the superficial differences, however, they share a recognizably similar approach: Readers (typically program faculty) are asked to evaluate sample texts and then to articulate the textual features that most influenced their ratings of individual texts. Participants then negotiate the textual features associated with different ratings into a system of assessment criteria that can be mapped into a visual-spatial representation of the program's writing values and, at least in theory, an assessment tool. The result is an entirely descriptive and context-sensitive measure of student success that effectively answers the question, "What do *we* value?"

With the exception of Stalions, whose interest in DCM seems to be in its descriptive power, the authors all report having selected DCM because they believed that its privileging of local control and its ability to derive assessment criteria from local practices would produce greater faculty support for the end result than would be possible using external assessment. And, indeed, all four projects seem to have produced a consistently high level of faculty buy-in. However, these projects also reveal one of DCM's most significant weaknesses. By distilling assessment criteria entirely from the values held by program faculty, the philosophy of DCM dictates an inward-looking culture that offers little scope for addressing questions about the appropriateness of local values. In some programs (presumably including all of those represented here), DCM's intentional and principled rejection of the outward-looking question "What *should* we value in student writing?" will be mitigated by participants whose own orientation toward a larger disciplinary affiliation will bring external values to bear on in-house evaluation. However, one of the realities of large-scale writing programs (including the four described in this collection) is that the majority of composition instruction is by adjunct and graduate student faculty whose grounding in composition pedagogy is necessarily limited. In a program of that kind, deriving assessment criteria entirely from local values might produce results of questionable value for shaping program goals. Regardless of the experience of program participants, however, the extent to which Broad and his co-authors treat privileging the local as an orthodoxy should give readers pause. The isolation of programs within the silos of local values seems likely to work at least as quickly toward the disintegration of higher education as anything that assessment by external agencies could do. The fact that the authors do not mention the need for program assessment to address extra-local as well as local contexts does not, of course, mean that they are not sensitive to it; but readers venturing into assessment for the first time should seek additional advice on the matter of local versus extra-local concerns in the assessment process.

In *What We Really Value,* Broad's rejection of prescriptive, external values—and the kind of assessment instruments in which external values can be enacted—results in a wholesale rejection of the idea of the rubric as a tool for assessing writing. Broad's use of the term rubric as a shorthand for all the ways that writing assessment can fail to address local realities, elide complexity, and allow powerful interests to generate self-serving data in the name of educational excellence is the most serious shortcoming of his earlier work. Broad himself seems to have recognized and taken some steps toward rectifying that problem (nothing as emphatic as a retraction, but an attempt at rapprochement) in his introduction to the current volume. Unfortunately his original error is reproduced in subsequent chapters as contributors sedulously avoid the "R" word without, in fact, being able to avoid producing structures that look remarkably like rubrics. Since a rubric is, after all, merely a graphical representation of a program's writing values used for the purpose of enabling systematic assessment of student writing, a rubric seems to be the almost inevitable outcome of generating and then organizing criteria for evaluating writing. Although Broad hints at the strong conceptual similarities between his "criteria map" and everyone else's "rubric," this is a point that may cause serious confusion for readers not well versed in the literature of assessment, and it unfortunately (and, I think, unnecessarily) obscures the genuine usefulness of dynamic criteria mapping.

Understood as a process of eliciting values for student writing inductively through dialogue driven by collective evaluation of writing samples, DCM creates significant opportunities for faculty participants to engage in meaningful professional development related to teaching writing. Faculty who regularly engage in substantive conversations about what they value in student writing and why (such as the conversations that emerged during all five of these projects), in so doing clarify and reinforce both their own expectations for student writing and their understanding of what textual features produce the effects they value. In this way, DCM's home-grown assessment creates opportunities for faculty to close the feedback loop by taking their experience of engaging in assessment back into the classroom. This is certainly one of DCM's greatest strengths.

The fifth project included in this volume, Stalions's analysis of the criteria used by graduate student raters in Bowling Green State University's placement process, illustrates a different application of dynamic criteria mapping: its use in determining the extent to which the values enacted by evaluators are consistent with the values stated in program guidelines. In his analysis of placement-related statements made by four pairs of graduate student raters, Stalions found that of the categories of statements made most often, nearly all were drawn from stated program criteria.

As Stalions describes it, staffing for the assessment program he studied depended heavily on graduate students, a transient workforce with very limited opportunity to develop institutional memory. Given this context, the high level of consistency Stalions found between stated program criteria and the criteria actually employed by raters suggests a notably high level of success in communicating program criteria to new team members. However, Stalions's mapping of categories of placement-related statements reveals interesting differences in raters' application of and privileging of program criteria compared to contextual information about the courses. Where some pairs referred almost exclusively to textual elements, others included references to the courses into which students were to be placed and to evidence in the essays of students' attitudes toward or preparation for learning. This suggests interesting avenues for further research on the effects of rater's outside experiences in causing them to privilege some criteria over others in making placement decisions. And although Stalions's demonstration is more proof-of-concept than a new contribution to the literature on assessment, it does illustrate what seems to be a fruitful opportunity for similar studies in other programs.

Organic Writing Assessment will be of greatest interest to three kinds of readers: graduate students seeking research projects in composition; program directors seeking the answer to the question Stalions asks: "do we really value what we say we really value?" (122); and assessment coordinators seeking to begin a new or substantially remodeled assessment program with significant faculty buy-in. Readers should be aware that the authors make relatively limited reference to the literature on assessment in general and do occasionally seem to argue for best practices on a philosophical rather than evidential basis.

Pittsburg, KS

Works Cited

Broad, Bob. *What We Really Value: Beyond Rubrics in Teaching and Assessing Writing*. Logan: Utah State UP, 2003. Print.

Going Wireless: A Critical Exploration of Wireless and Mobile Technologies for Composition Teachers and Researchers, edited by Amy C. Kimme Hea. New York: Hampton, 2009. 376 pp.

Reviewed by Ronda L. Wery, Texas Tech University

The first collection of its kind, *Going Wireless* offers Rhetoric and

Composition teachers, scholars, and administrators a continuum of practical and theoretical perspectives on wireless and mobile technology use in computer and composition teaching and research. *Going Wireless* certainly is as advertised in the introduction. The book is, in fact, "a far-reaching, multivocal dialogue" that "takes on difficult issues of integration, use, and development" and is "neither celebratory nor reactionary" (10) regarding these technologies and their effects on instructors, students, teaching, and learning. Mobile and wireless technologies are explored critically—not oversimplified as neutral, evil, or heroic. While part I explores transforming our idea of instruction itself, part II looks closely at how teachers and students conceive of their roles in these new instructional environments. Part III provides descriptions of actual experiences in these new environments. Part IV examines the interaction of composition and space in mobile environments, while part V examines both theoretical and practical implications of portable research, teaching, and learning. One of the great strengths of this text is its rich balance of theory and practical application throughout. The only unfortunate aspect of this fine publication is no fault of its editor or contributors: print production schedules did not allow them to incorporate more recent wireless and mobile technologies, such as the iPad and the variety of e-readers now available, in their discussions. One can only applaud their bravery in the attempt to capture this (literally) moving target.

In part I "Refiguring Writing, Teaching, and Learning through Wireless and Mobile Technologies," Johnson-Eilola and Stuart A. Selber lead off with "The Changing Shapes of Writing: Rhetoric, New Media, and Composition." In response to compositionists who would eschew texting, instant messaging (IM), Twitter, and Facebook, Johnson-Eilola and Selber propose that the "changing shapes" of students' daily interactions with one another outside the classroom require a more inclusive theoretical framework, one that places emerging genres alongside more traditional forms of classroom discourse. They propose C3T (Context, Change, Content, and Tools) to reveal the rhetorical complexity of communications with new media and provide a heuristic for students analyzing a variety of communication situations. Likewise, in "Learning Unplugged," Teddi Fishman and Kathleen Blake Yancey ask readers to cease "othering" wireless and mobile communication technologies by recognizing their place in composition pedagogy. Fishman and Yancey invite compositionists to consider the potential benefits of the technologies students already embrace, noting that admitting the technological other requires recognition of the epistemological ramifications of ubiquitous, potentially infinite, information flow: "Access to multiple resources can expand, deepen, and complicate both what is known and how what is known *comes to be known*" (37).

In part II: "Examining Teacher and Student Subjectivities in the Age of Wireless and Mobile Technologies," potential changes in identity and power relations among teachers and students are explored. In "'A Whole New Breed of Student Out There': Wireless Technology Ads and Teacher Identity," Karla Saari Kitalong analyzes rhetorically the portrayals of teachers in wireless technology ads and educational technology periodicals, arguing that these representations constrain the identity potential of teachers and students. Kitalong proposes Stuart Selber's tripartite model of functional, critical, and rhetorical techno-literacy as a potential path out of this identity crisis and toward greater agency. Ryan M. Moeller, in "ReWriting Wi-Fi: The Surveillance of Mobility and Student Agency," identifies rhetorical appeals that blind us to the ubiquitous surveillance of wireless technologies. Moeller sees Berlin's social-epistemic rhetoric in the composition classroom as a means to restore teacher and student agency by interrogating the wireless world in which we work, play, and blur the lines between work and play. The final chapter in part II, Melinda Turnley's "Reterritorialized Flows: Critically Considering Student Agency in Wireless Pedagogies," encourages educators to reflect on the role of space (both physical and virtual) in writing instruction. Concerned that anywhere, anytime learning could lead to education that is decontextualized from larger cultural concerns, Turnley employs Deleuze and Guattari's concepts of deterritorialization and reterritorialization to emphasize motion and connection.

Part III, "Cutting the Cord: Stories on Wireless Teaching and Learning in the Composition Classroom," takes a more practical, less theoretical, approach than earlier sections of the book, providing a view of teachers and students in their local contexts. Will Hochman and Mike Palmquist's "From Desktop to Laptop: Making Transitions to Wireless Learning in Writing Classrooms" builds upon the 1998 *Transitions* study by Palmquist and others. The current study, based on instructor interviews and student surveys, explores not only how participants incorporate laptops into the writing classroom but how their attitudes toward technology and writing are shaped as a result of doing so. This research has implications for both computer-based and traditional classrooms.

In "Changing the Ground of Graduate Education: Wireless Laptops Bring Stability, Not Mobility, to Graduate Teaching Assistants [GTAs]," Kevin Brooks finds that wireless laptops improve the working conditions of GTAs, which has a positive effect on their students as well. Brooks also offers helpful arguments for WPAs seeking funding for similar initiatives. In "A Profile of Students Using Wireless Technologies in a First-Year Learning Community," Loel Kim, Susan L. Popham, Emily A. Thrush, Joseph G. Jones, and Donna J. Daulton offer up a case study of wireless use in a first-year cohort of nursing students. Mya Poe and Simson Garfinkel conclude part III with "Security and Privacy in the Wireless Classroom," wherein they discuss how to balance security needs with the freedom necessary to promote pedagogical innovation.

Part IV, "Teaching and Learning in Motion: Mobility and Pedagogies of Space," confronts the theoretical intersection among space, mobility, composition, and wireless communication environments. In "Perpetual Contact: Articulating the Anywhere, Anytime Pedagogical Model of Mobile Composing," Amy C. Kimme Hea employs articulation theory to explore and critique the "cultural narratives of ubiquity" enabled by wireless technologies. Hea first examines arguments that uncritically tout the value of anywhere, anytime computing, and then problematizes those narratives in terms of two real-world initiatives—one global, one local. Hea calls for praxis in teaching and research, based on a non-utopian, critical recognition that even technologies that seem "determined" to empower can, in fact, constrain both teachers and learners.

In "Writing in the Wild: A Paradigm for Mobile Composition," Olin Bjork and John Pedro Schwartz answer Geoffrey Sirc's call to consider composition sites outside traditional composing spaces, while Nicole Brown, in "Metaphors of Mobility: Emerging Spaces for Rhetorical Reflection and Communication," responds to Kathleen Blake Yancey's call "for the socially aware remediation of text to create new and dynamic genres and literacies" (249). Brown proposes that graffiti and other public forms of art can serve as useful metaphors for teaching and learning with mobile technologies.

In part V, "Teaching and Research in My Pocket: Mobile Gadgets and Portable Practices," Clay Spinuzzi leads off with "The Genie's Out of the Bottle: Leveraging Mobile and Wireless Technologies in Qualitative Research." Spinuzzi first traces the evolution of citizen journalism made possible by smart phones and other portable video devices. He then issues a wake-up call to qualitative researchers in Composition and Rhetoric: What has happened to professional journalists could happen to us. What if research participants decided to use their own mobile devices to analyze the researchers—to watch the watchers? He argues effectively that instead of responding with fear and defensiveness, researchers could view mobile devices as an opportunity to involve our participants more deeply in the research process and, thereby, tell a more complete story.

Dene Girgar and John F. Barber, in "Winged Words: On the Theory and Use of Internet Radio," attempts to overcome visual-centric approaches to literacy to reveal how the spoken word can enrich rhetorical and critical perspectives and provide a unique contribution to literacy. Continuing in an aural vein, in "Dancing with the iPod: Navigating the New Wireless Landscape of Composition Studies," Beth Martin and Lisa Meloncon Posner interpose song lyrics and analysis to reveal a "mobile landscape" for students and teachers to navigate while critically considering the impact of mobile devices on human lives both inside and outside the classroom.

The book also includes an appendix by David Menchaca, who defines key terms and distinguishes the separate histories of "wireless" and "mobile," suggesting that having a grasp of the history of the technologies we use daily enables teachers, students, and researchers to be more critical consumers of said technologies.

This groundbreaking collection of essays explores the evolution of teacher, student, and researcher agency and identity during a pivotal time in higher education. In the end, this anthology not only traces the theoretical and pedagogical implications of applying the latest technologies to composition, it reveals the evolving relationships among human beings who communicate with one another through those technologies.

Lubbock, TX

Walking and Talking Feminist Rhetorics: Landmark Essays and Controversies, edited by Lindal Buchanan and Kathleen J. Ryan. West Lafayette: Parlor, 2010. 483 pp.

Reviewed by Nancy Myers, University of North Carolina at Greensboro

When I read a draft of the introduction to *Walking and Talking Feminist Rhetorics: Landmark Essays and Controversies* last summer, I was eager to see the collection in print. The draft introduction suggested an anthology of scholarly abundance and possibility. This collection has not disappointed, as Lindal Buchanan and Kathleen J. Ryan bring together in one text a nuanced understanding of feminist rhetorics as an established dynamic field. They have included 29 primarily women's but also men's voices in a multivalent scholarly exchange that has been occurring over the last twenty years. The editors define the field of feminist rhetorics as a community of scholars and body of scholarship with an intellectual, theoretical, practical, and political agenda that "encourages others to think, believe, and act in ways that promote equal treatment and opportunities for women" (xiv). The significance of *Walking and Talking Feminist Rhetorics* is in its selection and arrangement of valuable contemporary articles that mark a middle ground between rhetorical traditions and interdisciplinary impulses for the discipline of Rhetoric and Composition Studies. Additionally, it provides a starting point for women and men who are interested in promoting social equity in their academic and professional endeavors.

The 26 previously published articles, book excerpts, reviews, and rejoinders are divided into four sections: 1) feminist rhetorics' beginnings, 2) its methods and methodologies, 3) its genres and styles, and 4) its controversies presented as case studies. In the collection's introduction, Buchanan and Ryan focus on their metaphors of walking and talking in this interdisciplinary field as emblematic of their textual choices. Walking allows for a combination of "intellectual flexibility and openness" and "reflexivity and curiosity," while talking represents the collaborative aspects of their work (xiv). Enacting what they are walking and talking about, two of the case study introductions are written by graduate students, Samuel R. Evans and Barbara Hebert. The editors' introduction, along with Kate Ronald's foreword and the introductory comments to the four divisions provide context and insight to their choices of texts. While the scholarly claim of landmark as "ground-breaking" or "innovative" always implies the risky terrain of judgment and criteria, the term also means "signpost" or "marker" referring to a topographical location. It is that second meaning that the editors suggest when they refer to their choices of selections and arrangement as their "journey to this point in time" within the field of feminist rhetorics (xv). In their mapping of the field, they distinguish five research strands that wind through the four sections. Each strand offers alternative theories, criteria, methods, and readings: a) recovery of women rhetors and rhetoricians, b) analyses of the contextual network of forces in women's rhetorics, c) examinations of "gender bias" in rhetorical traditions, d) critiques of "foundational disciplinary concepts," and e) interrogations of established epistemologies and "research practices" (xviii-xix). Another contextual field marker is the brief historical trajectory of patriarchal rhetoric that establishes the editors' beginning point of the field of feminist rhetorics as the 1989 publication of Karlyn Kohrs Campbell's *Man Cannot Speak for Her*.

The first three sections of the collection focus on the topics, purposes, and practices of the field of feminist rhetorics, while the fourth section highlights some key debates about them. Part 1, "Charting the Emergence of Feminist Rhetorics," establishes the field by exploring the crossing of feminism with rhetoric, so it focuses on the initial research questions and approaches in texts published between 1989 and 1995 and includes texts by Campbell, Cheryl Glenn, Susan C. Jarratt, Krista Ratcliffe, and a collaboratively written piece by Lisa Ede, Cheryl Glenn, and Andrea Lunsford. For instance, the 1995 "Border Crossings: Intersections of Rhetoric and Feminism" reconsiders the five traditional canons of rhetoric in light of women's ways of knowing and speaking and argues for the revising and nuancing of established principles in both feminist and rhetorical theories through the interweaving of the two fields. Part 2, "Articulating and Enacting Feminist Methods and Methodologies," examines feminist historiography and the ways that it both shapes and draws attention to "women's rhetorical interests, experiences, and accomplishments" (110). The six journal articles by Patricia Bizzell, Vicki Tolar Collins (Burton), Jessica Enoch, Mary Queen, Susan Romano, and Hui Wu demonstrate the historical scope, ethnic/racial diversity, and transnational approaches of the field's topics. For example, employing feminist rhetorical *topoi* as sites for recovery, Romano presents four alternative narratives of a sixteenth-century Spanish female missionary's disappearance in Mexico. In contrast, Queen develops a digital methodology to explore rhetorically the political motives involved in the online representations of Afghan women's bodies and voices post 9/11. Part 3, "Exploring Gendered Sites, Genres, and Styles of Rhetoric," concentrates on women's historical locations and situations and the ways in which their rhetorical agency is contained and enacted. Chronologically organized by topic, these six historical arguments provided by Jane Donawerth, Bonnie J. Dow and Mari Boor Tonn, Nan Johnson, Shirley Wilson Logan, Carol Mattingly, and Susan Zaeske examine women's rhetorical options, challenges, and innovations from the seventeenth through twentieth centuries. As illustration, "Black Women on the Speaker's Platform (1832-1899)" details the various issues and topics, in addition to slavery, that American black women organized around, fought to change, and spoke to during the nineteenth century. These include "employment, civil rights, woman's rights, emigration, and self-improvement" as well as "mob violence, racial uplift, and support for the southern black woman" (254).

The abundance of women writing about women's rhetoric is simultaneously reinforced and altered in the fourth section. Part 4, "Examining Controversies," is a series of four case studies tied to specific controversies revolving around the debated issues of a) recovery or critique as the field's primary objective, b) rhetorical aims and their impact, c) women's roles in curricular reform, and d) rhetorical historiography. The first case study that questions whether women can be placed in the rhetorical canon pairs Barbara Biesecker's critique of Campbell's *Man Cannot Speak for Her* with Campbell's response and defense. The second case study questions whether or not there are "distinct masculine and feminine communication styles" and includes Sonja K. Foss and Cindy L. Griffin's article on invitational rhetoric and Celeste Michelle Condit's critique and argument for women's persuasive rhetoric (360). In the third case study, Roxanne Mountford's book review criticizes Robert J. Connors's historical account of rhetorical education's demise due to women entering college during the nineteenth century as oversimplistic, biased, and stereotypic, calling into question his method and methodology. The final case study begins with Xin Liu Gale's critical analysis of feminist research methods used by Glenn and Jarratt and Rory Ong pertaining to Aspasia of Miletus. The rejoinders of Glenn and Jarratt follow. The editors' choice to include these four debates reinforces and remaps the questions and perspectives of the first three sections of the collection and continues the conversation beyond the collections' texts. For example, the short introductions to the case studies suggest this continuation by listing other texts directly affecting or related to the controversy. In addition, the issue of rhetorical aims and the question "Is persuasion violence?" could be enhanced and extended by reading Sally Gearhart's 1979 "The Womanization of Rhetoric" and Jarratt's 1991 "Feminism and Composition: The Case for Conflict."

Multivocality is apparent not only in these scholarly debates but also in the number of bibliographic citations involved in this type of collection. Each of the reprinted texts includes its original citations. The Works Cited for the collection's and sections' introductions is yet another rich list. Additionally, the editors have compiled a selected bibliography of influential monographs, edited collections, anthologies, and special journal issues focused on feminist rhetorics.

The variety of competing and complementary voices and the editors' careful attention to and fine distinctions of scholarly exchange and alternative views invite ample opportunities and possibilities for this collection's use. I can see *Walking and Talking Feminist Rhetorics* used in upper-level undergraduate courses and graduate courses in Rhetoric and Composition studies and in Women and Gender Studies. Moreover, it can easily be supplemented with articles referred to but not included. At the graduate level and depending on the focus of the Rhetoric and Composition studies seminar, I might pair this text with Eileen E. Schell and K. J. Rawson's *Rhetorica in Motion: Feminist Rhetorical Methods and Methodologies*, Kate Ronald and Joy Ritchie's *Teaching Rhetorica: Theory, Pedagogy, Practice*, or one of the feminism and composition collections. The value of the case studies is twofold, both pedagogical. The first is the discussion about the debate and the added research and reading that can happen to extend the voices in it. The second is that these debates operate as models for a case study assignment with students choosing their own issues to explore. At $40 for the paperback and $30 for the Adobe eBook, this collection offers our discipline a strong, usable text at a price we can work with in our courses.

Greensboro, NC

Works Cited

Campbell, Karlyn Kohrs. *Man Cannot Speak for Her*. 2 vols. New York: Praeger, 1989. Print.

Gearhart, Sally Miller. "The Womanization of Rhetoric." *Women's Studies International Quarterly* 2 (1979): 195-201. Print.

Jarratt, Susan C. "Feminism and Composition: The Case for Conflict." *Contending with Words: Composition and Rhetoric in a Postmodern Age*. Ed. Patricia Harkin and John Schilb. New York: MLA, 1991. 105-23. Print.

Ronald, Kate, and Joy Ritchie, eds. *Teaching Rhetorica: Theory, Pedagogy, Practice*. Portsmouth: Heinemann/Boynton/Cook, 2006. Print.

Schell, Eileen E., and K. J. Rawson, ed. *Rhetorica in Motion: Feminist Rhetorical Methods and Methodologies*. Pittsburgh: U of Pittsburgh P, 2010. Print.

Contributors

Christine Peters Cucciarre is an Assistant Professor at the University of Delaware. She is also a mother to her four-year-old son, Pace. Her research interests include creative writing pedagogy, composition pedagogy, WAC, and now, alternative models for tenure and teaching faculty.

Robert Danberg is a Visiting Assistant Professor in the Binghamton University Writing Initiative. He received his PhD from Syracuse University's Composition and Cultural Rhetoric Program in 2010. His scholarly interests include theories of knowledge; teaching and learning in writing classrooms and across disciplines; teacher education; and Jewish Rhetoric. His poems have appeared in *Ploughshares, The Sun, The Cortland Review* and other publications online and in print.

Loren Loving Marquez is an Assistant Professor of English at Salisbury University in Salisbury, Maryland. She teaches graduate courses in composition theory and pedagogy, mentors graduate teaching assistants, teaches advanced composition, and directs the First-Year Writing Program. She is mother to Nate, 4, and Libby, 1.

Deborah E. Morris is the proud mother of two incredible undergraduate students and is herself a doctoral student in Bowling Green State University's Rhetoric & Writing Program. She is an adjunct instructor of writing at Ivy Tech Community College Northeast and enjoys research in composition pedagogy, formative assessment, and student motivation.

Lee Nickoson greatly enjoys being mother to five-year-old Olivia. Lee also enjoys teaching and studying all-things related to writing research and pedagogy at Bowling Green State University, where she is an assistant professor of English and member of the Rhetoric & Writing Program.

A mother of two young children, **Kim Hensley Owens** is also Assistant Professor of Writing and Rhetoric at the University of Rhode Island. Her recent publications include an *Inside Higher Ed* career-advice essay, a chapter in the edited collection *Textual Mothers/Maternal Texts,* and articles in *Pedagogy, Enculturation,* and *Written Communication.*

Kelly Ritter is Associate Professor of English and Director of Composition at UNC-Greensboro, and author of *Before Shaugnessy: Basic Writing at Yale and Harvard, 1920-1960* (SIU Press, 2009) and *Who Owns School? Authority, Students, and Online Discourse* (Hampton Press, 2010). Her next book, *To Know Her Own History: Writing at the Woman's College, 1943-1963*, is forthcoming from the University of Pittsburgh Press.

Todd Ruecker is a doctoral candidate in rhetoric and composition at the University of Texas at El Paso, with a focus on second language writing. He has published book reviews in various journals and has had articles accepted for publication in journals such as *ELT Journal* and *Critical Inquiry in Language Studies*.

Mary P. Sheridan is an Associate Professor at the University of Wyoming. She has authored *Girls, Feminism, and Grassroots Literacies*, co-authored *Design Literacies*, and has published in *Kairos, Written Communication, Computers and Composition,* and *Journal of Basic Writing*. Mary P. is the mother of three fabulous children.

Call for Proposals – 2011 Graduate Research Network

The **Graduate Research Network (GRN)** invites proposals for its 2011 workshop, May 19, 2011, at the Computers and Writing Conference hosted by the University of Michigan. The C&W Graduate Research Network is an all-day pre-conference event, open to all registered conference participants at no charge. Roundtable discussions group those with similar interests and discussion leaders who facilitate discussion and offer suggestions for developing research projects and for finding suitable venues for publication. We encourage anyone interested or involved in graduate education and scholarship—students, professors, mentors, and interested others—to participate in this important event. The GRN welcomes those pursuing work at any stage, from those just beginning to consider ideas to those whose projects are ready to pursue publication. Participants are also invited to apply for travel funding through the CW/GRN Travel Grant Fund.

Deadline for submissions is **April 25, 2011**. For more information or to submit a proposal, visit our Web site at:

http://class.georgiasouthern.edu/writling/GRN/2011/index.html

or email jwalker@georgiasouthern.edu.

Walk-ins welcome.

DEPAUL UNIVERSITY
Chicago, IL

Department of
WRITING, RHETORIC, & DISCOURSE

Master of Arts Degrees in
New Media Studies
Writing, Rhetoric, & Discourse
with concentrations in
Professional and Technical Writing
Teaching Writing & Language

Graduate Certificate Program in TESOL

Faculty
Matthew Abraham, Julie Bokser, Darsie Bowden, Antonio Ceraso, René De los Santos, Lisa Dush, Sarah Read, Christine Tardy, Peter Vandenberg

wrd.depaul.edu WRD

www.ingramcontent.com/pod-product-compliance
Lightning Source LLC
Chambersburg PA
CBHW031632160426
43196CB00006B/384